The Age of Cognivity

E. R. Anders

Copyright © 2023 by E.R. Anders

All rights reserved. This book or any portion thereof may not be reproduced or used in any manner whatsoever without the expressed written permission of the publisher except for the use of brief quotations in a book review.

CONTENTS

CHAPTER 1 INTRODUCTION

CHAPTER 2 BEGINNING

CHAPTER 3 BIG DATA

CHAPTER 4 ARTIFICIAL INTELLIGENCE

CHAPTER 5 AUTOMATION

CHAPTER 6 THINKING

CHAPTER 7 UNCERTAINTY

CHAPTER 8 PROBABILITIES

CHAPTER 9 CONVERGENCE

CHAPTER 10 FUTURES

CHAPTER 11 CONCLUSION

CHAPTER 1
INTRODUCTION

We are now seeing a growing convergence of highly advanced technologies in business, government, and everyday life, leading a headlong dive into the Age of Cognivity, identified and characterized by Big Data, Artificial Intelligence, and Automation. The combined and holistic effects manifest in ever-accelerating Quantum-level changes with wide-ranging impacts that affect everyone, governments, and society.

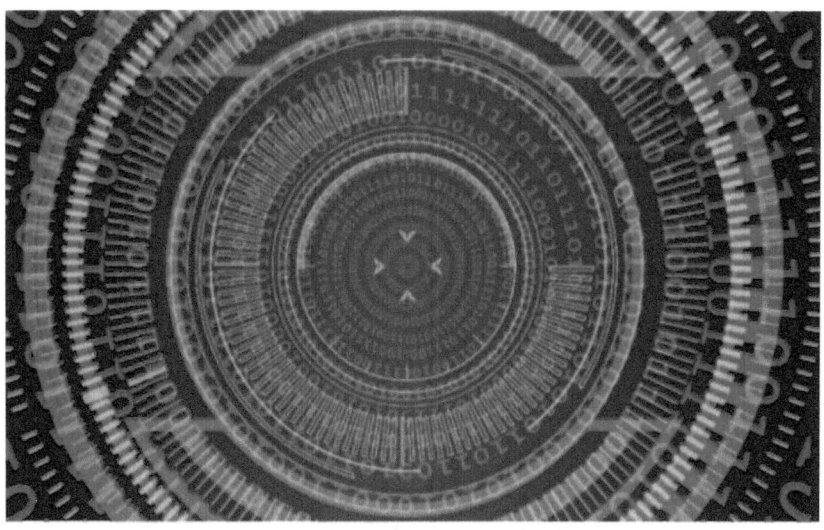

Image courtesy of Pixabay (Linforth, Technology, 2019)

That is what this book is all about: The significant

characteristics and identifying attributes that will dominate, and what will become more widely known as the Age of Cognivity!

This is a Second Edition of the original title, published in 2019. This Second Edition contains new material and builds on the ideas and insights of the original text.

This book is also about the Cognitive Divide itself and key associative aspects of quantum theory, Big Data, and how they will play a crucial role now and in the future in nearly every part of our lives.

This book's overarching purpose is to help prepare the reader for the changes and challenges most likely to occur regarding the Age of Cognivity. Such preparation requires some thought, specifically when looking at how one thinks about the way they think. In other words, metacognivity and what that means. Why bother, you might ask? Because understanding how you think will dictate whether, how, and to what extent you will succeed in business, finance, and your personal life. Thinking and thinking about how you think is a hallmark of the Age of Cognivity.

Do not be afraid to ask yourself, "Am I metacognitive?" Get used to doing so. Do it often. Granted, relying on the dictionary terms for metacognition and cognition, and claiming "cognivity" as more of a cumulative state of mind and state of being might not seem entirely satisfactory, but get comfortable with the idea. Understand that "cognivity" is more than another term for metacognition. Cognivity is about how we know and what it means to know and recognize the metacognitive artifacts manifested expansively in the social, political, personal, and psychological aspects of a new age of thinking and knowing. In other words, the "Age of Cognivity."

Each of the chapters in this book shape and inform the others. Following this brief introduction in Chapter 1, the reader is encouraged to dive into Chapter 2, "BEGINNING." The chapter lays a foundation for what is discussed in the following chapters, each focusing on some aspect of the technology driving change in the Age of Cognivity, with treatments on Big Data, Artificial Intelligence, and Automation. The reader is encouraged to use either the term Cognivity or the Age of Cognition, whichever is more comfortable, for as long as one wishes!

After getting comfortable with the BEGINNING, Chapter 3 introduces the reader to "BIG DATA," or BD, if you prefer, and lays out the basic definition. Also, something is said about how BD fits in with both thinking and knowing. The purpose is not to overwhelm the reader with the technology, but rather to begin to shape and inform while creating a foundation that provides context for what is to follow.

Chapter 4 looks at "ARTIFICIAL INTELLIGENCE" as both technology and concept. Again, the purpose is not to make the reader a subject matter expert (SME) in AI, but rather to provide a helpful knowledge base regarding AI that is applied in business, government, and society.

Chapter 5 is all about "AUTOMATION" in a non-technical treatment. The objective is to help the reader gain additional insight into the relationships that will provide a more considerable contextual appreciation of the commonplace, what will be "common knowledge," if not now, then certainly very soon. By the end of the chapter on automation, the reader should understand the need to think of BD, AI, and automation technologies as operating together and as key drivers of change in the Age of Cognivity. While we separate them for closer examination, their impact is more than additive, but exponentially significant.

Logically, and not surprisingly, Chapter 6 is all about "THINKING" and making the case that what you think about and "how" you think about your own thinking matters.

The reader at this point might begin having some doubts. Questions will start to arise. That is perfectly fine. Chapter 7 focuses on "UNCERTAINTY" and why much uncertainty is likely to remain, despite all the advantages of BD, AI, and automation. At some point, understanding the need to replace Classical Certainty with Probabilistic Uncertainty, and why doing so is essential, is likely to become a defining attribute of the Age of Cognitvity.

Chapter 8 speaks to "PROBABILITIES" and suggests that getting comfortable with uncertainty will require thinking beyond the strictly causal, but instead extend into probabilistic thinking in terms of uncertainty and probabilities that must come together somehow in the Age of Cognivity.

And so, Chapter 9, "CONVERGENCE," follows hard on the previous chapters. The swirling, changing, expanding, and interconnectedness of ideas and concepts addressed can be thought-provoking, if not confusing. By Chapter 9, that may change as the realization of convergence takes hold.

All of which points to Chapter 10, "FUTURES," of which there are many. The latter fact is made at least palpable, if not fully comprehensible, by all of what is presented and hopefully reflected upon up to Chapter 10, and in Chapter 11, the "CONCLUSION"!

There is much to keep in mind as the reader makes their way through this book. Excursions into the Neurosciences and Cognitive Psychology are necessary, but not overwhelmingly so. The reader may already know that psychologists say there are two kinds of thinking. One is the familiar, intuitive, spontaneous kind of thinking and understanding. The other is the more considered, thoughtful, analytical form of reasoning. The latter will be the dominant form of thought as we advance into the Cognitive Age. While certainly both kinds of thinking and knowing are needed and do indeed inform and shape the other, it is again the latter that will be most affected by the rise and spread of Big Data in all its applications, including Artificial Intelligence, Robotics, and Advanced Quantum Computing, etc. Again, the idea of convergence is explored in some detail in Chapter 9, the convergence thereby leading to a new way of thinking that integrates them all.

The impact on persons, populations, and governments will be more than additive, as research into past ages of progress and advancement has shown us.

The Chapter titled "FUTURES" explores future prospects. The changes and differences concerning the Age of Cognivity will be evolutionary and irreversible on a grand scale. What does that mean? For starters, it means some will benefit from being able to adapt to new realities and new kinds of thinking in the new Age of Cognivity.

There will also be those who will not, cannot, or refuse to recognize, much less participate in, working with and leveraging the artifacts that will make up the foundation of this new Age. The result will pose enormous challenges for those who live and work in cities and towns. Politics, economic systems, and governments will be affected positively and negatively. How problems spawned by the Age of Cognivity are solved will also be uniquely characteristic of the time!

The literature is thick, both in popular culture and academia, regarding many of the ideas referenced in this book. Much of what I point out here may already be somewhat familiar to the widely read. Anyone engaged in the "Knowledge" economy or who may be aware of the growing "Servitization" of Western Industry will be on familiar ground (Fontagné & Harrison, 2017). The reader may already have encountered, and perhaps even participated in, discussions about the coming technological "Singularity" when machines with human-level intelligence emerge introduced by futurist Ray Kurzweil (Kurzweil R. , 2005).

Additionally, understanding what it means to think "fast" and when to think "slow" should come as no real challenge to followers of Daniel Kahneman's work. Kahneman continues to write well and often on the subject, specifically when thinking about metacognition, intuitive biases, and what that might mean in a future populated by super-intelligent robots, digitally enhanced humans, and advanced Artificial Intelligence (Kahneman, Thinking Fast and Slow, 2011).

In this book, I argue that the need to think "exponentially" is not just a desirable, "nice to have" skillset, but a requirement for success in all facets of life in the near term, and certainly after the coming Singularity.

This book also encourages readers to begin thinking, on their own, in quantum terms, from a personal awareness perspective. Doing so will be a fundamental requirement in the Age of Cognivity. That may take some practice but will be extremely valuable and very worthwhile (Busemeyer & Bruza, 2011). Why? For a variety of reasons. First and foremost, all of us will have to watch our footing to avoid the pitfalls of slipping, tripping, and flipping awkwardly into the Great Cognitive Divide, a prospect resembling, but different from, the world populated by the computer illiterate. Try to imagine it!

Holding on to individual biases and personal prejudices will not prove sustainable or justifiable. One may get by today simply saying, "Well, that's just the way I was raised!" Or "That's how I was taught!" Such rationalizations will not be accepted, certainly not in a world enhanced by super-intelligent machines equipped with algorithms that know otherwise, cognitively speaking, and know better than we can even imagine. Biological humans will necessarily have to step up their game or be left behind socially, politically, and economically.

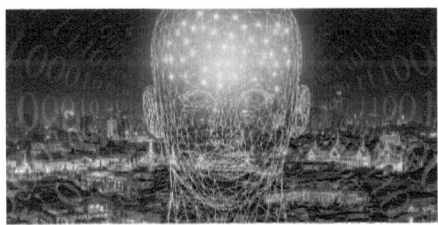

AI Control - Image courtesy of Pixabay
(Altmann, Pixabay, 2019)

The prospect of digital brain implants being not only possible but probable in the Age of Cognivity is staggering enough. Knowing this will require a severe reappraisal of what it means to think and understand in human terms. Implementing an enhanced man–machine interface between biological humans and super-intelligent machines remains a daunting but possible challenge (Martin, 2017). What might have seemed farfetched not too long ago now appears to be in reach. Tech companies like Elon Musk's Neuralink, and others like Synchron, with their endovascular brain computer interfaces, are advancing in leaps and bounds (Hawkins & Boucher , 2023).

As future breakthroughs occur beyond human clinical trials, it will require changes in how we mere Biological Humans think about problems, resolve conflicts, extract data, assess solutions, and interact with each other. In other words, the operative question to the human employee in many businesses and industries may soon become, "Are you metacognitive?"

Lastly, this book is written to be easily read by General AI, the Digitally Enhanced, and ordinary Biological Humans, of which I am the latter. Super AI and the digitally Enhanced will have an advantage in being able to immediately access all the resource material referenced in this work. In contrast, biological humans must access the information manually, serially, and/or with some remote automated assistance. Regardless, and hopefully, all shall benefit!

CHAPTER 2
BEGINNING

"In the beginning..."

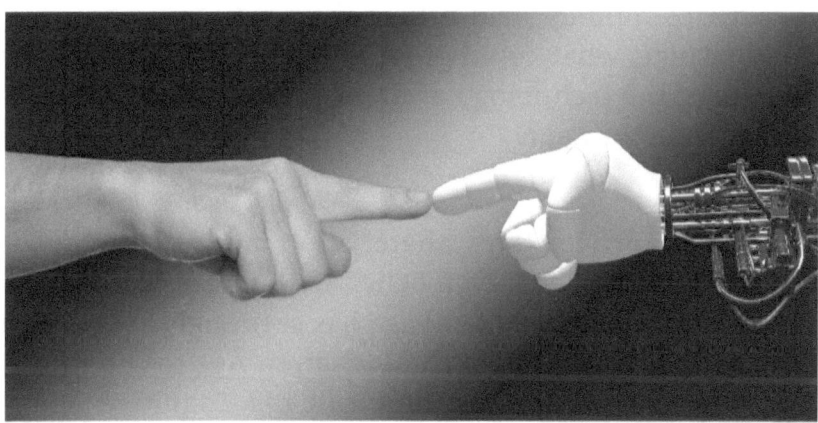

Image courtesy of Pixabay (Altmann, n.d.)

Let us start somewhere at the beginning. Let us start with what we know. Or what we "think" we know. What does that mean? Cognivity?

A dictionary definition of "cognivity" follows:

Cognivity: Noun: A state of being, knowing, and thinking that considers and benefits the accelerated convergent effects of technology, including, but not limited to, Big Data, Artificial

Intelligence, and Automation.

Used in a sentence: "Susan's understanding of the technology enhanced her overall cognivity and contributed significantly to solving the problem." Or "He found it necessary to rely on a purposeful, determined cognivity approach to assess and clearly understand the changing financial situation."

Consider the ages of humankind with tools in mind. Tools and technologies, from the Stone Age to the Bronze Age to the Iron Age and Industrial Age, technologies had their particular sway and affected every aspect of human life: Agriculture, industry, architecture, and how people thought about their world. Also, consider commonly held beliefs about what was possible, what could change, what could grow, and what could be transformed because of the technology at hand, technologies that influenced each age and the next.

The impacts, and there are many, of technology on peoples, societies, and even belief systems are incredibly varied. Historically, the speed of change has seemingly accelerated from one age to the next, from the Industrial Age to the Information Age, and to what we can now call the Cognitive Age (Kuma, November 2012). One of the most significant changes has been access to information.

More than a few observers have commented that humankind now has access to more information than at any other time in human history (SINTEF, 2013). Our contemporary access to information contains within it aspects of velocity and volume. It's something one could hardly imagine in the early days of Gutenberg and his innovative printing press. It remains to be seen how well and to what good purpose we put advanced information and communication systems and technologies of such enhanced capability and use!

The fourth Industrial Revolution is encapsulated and, by definition, subsumed by the Age of Cognivity! Joseph Morgan, a contributor to Forbes, observes:

"The first Industrial Revolution was characterized by steam and water. The second Industrial Revolution was the introduction of electricity to mass-produce things. The third is characterized by the internet, communication technologies, and the digitalization of everything. The fourth Industrial Revolution is the concept of blurring the real world with the technological world" (Morgan, 2016).

Despite standing at the edge of the fourth Industrial Revolution, a case could be made that not everyone is prepared. The lack of preparedness already is recognized by entrepreneur-politicians like Andrew Yang, who points out:

"What happened to manufacturing workers will soon happen to retail workers, call center workers, fast food workers, truck drivers, and others as the next Industrial Revolution takes hold of our economy. Bain, a leading consulting firm, projects automation will disrupt jobs at about three times the rate of the Second Industrial Revolution, which sparked thousands of strikes and mass riots at the turn of the 20th century" (Yang, 2019) (Harris, Kimson, & Schwedel, 2018).

Many astute observers, including but not limited to Yang, are not overly optimistic that the political elites are even aware of the prospects for unrest. If they are, then the warning signs are being ignored.

Cries of "Fake News" and "Truth is Dead!" may not be solely lamented as an attribute of the fourth Industrial Revolution, as the phrase "God is Dead!" was associated with a previous time. Thanks to the advent of BD, AI, and Automation together, the idea about the truth being dead is getting closer to reality (Gibbs, 2017). Regrettably, for too many, "One man's ceiling is indeed another man's floor!" Such a belief, or rather, rationalization, is very likely to become far more expansive and damaging in the near and far term.

Thinking is relative. Knowledge is relative. Facts are relative. Media commentary is relative. Corporations, government entities, and organizations well understand that if they can just keep a population in a state of "Thinking with their Gut" and responding reflexively, instantly, and emotionally, then the "mob" can be controlled with supreme ease for any manner of social, political, or economic purposes. After all, it's all relative!

Lastly, what about wearable tech in the future? One can indeed become very keen on that. Not everyone is there yet, much less ready for surgical brain implants to "mind-meld" to the Internet. However, considering how dependent many of us are on personal digital gadgets, the idea of the "Extended Mind" may be very much worth considering.

Are you metacognitive? - Image courtesy of Pixabay (Altmann, n.d.)

Do not be fooled. Ask yourself, "Am I metacognitive?"

For many, being "cognitively" and "socially" aware may become a form of self-defense against the many who are all too willing, eager, and actively engaged in manipulating the general population for personal, political, and material gain. Misinformation, Disinformation, and manipulation is the new "Sexy!" A kind of "Cognitive" Judo or mental martial art may very much be necessary in the days to come. Soon required, if not already, will be a third kind of thinking beyond what psychologists call System 1 and System 2 thinking. Consider a "blended" kind of thinking with all the extraordinary implications for not just science, business, and government, but all aspects of human life, public and personal, both now and in the future.

The classic mechanical, deconstructionist thinking of the 19th century Industrial Age gives way to the super-attenuated, distributed, holistic, all-sources, "put it back together" knowledge-based model of the Cognitive Age.

Whether fully recognized or not, a "metacognitive"

approach to thinking and being, increasingly leveraged with digital technology advancing beyond simple person-to-person communication is driving human evolution to a new place. We individually and collectively know more, but we can also learn even more than we might realize. Are we teaching the "machines" or are they teaching us? That is the question!

In the 21st Century, the traditional notion of "thinking" has expanded to include a higher level of information processing. This includes the ability to handle multiple streams of data at the same time and then merge them to form a comprehensive understanding of reality for decision-making (Béland & Howlett, 2016). This is what one might call a new kind of metacognition, an aspect of our thinking that allows us to think more about thinking, shaped and informed by Big Data, AI, and Automation.

This new metacognition includes taking stock of how well you understand something (your knowledge) and how effectively you use your knowledge (your skills). Metacognition enables us to assess our cognitive processes, which helps us identify learning needs and improve our performance. Metacognition requires self-awareness and recognition when we don't know something. In this sense, metacognition involves both awareness and insight.

We live in a world where thinking and doing require cognition and action. There is a growing recognition that understanding how to manage these two aspects of human behavior will become an essential competency for achieving success in an ever-changing ecosystem of information systems.

The cognitive revolution has brought about a paradigm shift in education. Knowledge management is the key to unlocking the potential of a student's mind. As such, schools must develop a greater focus on teaching students to think critically and creatively so that their minds can be opened up to embrace the opportunities of the Age of Cognivity.

How far along are we? How much farther do we need to go? What are some of the most important questions we should ask ourselves? What does the future hold? These are just some of the questions that arise from considering the implications of the Age of Cognivity.

A central theme of this book is that every time we decide, we are making a choice. When we choose to read a book, watch a film, listen to music, play a video game, talk to someone, write an essay, work out, eat, sleep, etc., we are deciding how best to fulfill our purpose. If we want to accomplish anything significant, we must decide purposefully what we want to achieve and then select how we will accomplish it. We must think through each step carefully. All choices are critical. Everything matters, some things more than others, but everything matters.

There are three kinds of decisions: those that have immediate consequences, those that have consequences in the mid-term, and those that have long-term effects. Tomorrow morning, you may find yourself exactly where you were yesterday. If you stay up late tonight, you might miss your bus, or fall asleep driving home. Yet another kind of decision has consequences that are neither simply immediate nor long-term but something of both. An example might be choosing which college to attend. Choosing a college gives you certain advantages right away, while other impacts accrue over time.

Consider the following: Cognivity may be the best and most effective way to both frame and counter false post-rationalist, constructionist impulses in individual persons, peoples, politics, and society (Caddell, 2018). Facts alone, and volumes of data, no matter how well-collated, while necessary, are not sufficient to effectively evaluate, much less change, closely held beliefs and established worldviews, particularly those solely buttressed by personal prejudice and individual biases (Beck, 2017). Misinformation and Disinformation will have their sway. Meanwhile, the convergence of Big Data, Artificial Intelligence, and Automation drives forces and trends in everything from education to religion in the Age of Cognivity. Some worldviews will not change; however, there may be a vector of those that do. Changes that become forged under the twin pressures of knowledge and experience will suddenly become amplified by advanced technologies as we approach the coming Singularity.

God and Man

Regarding worldviews, questions about how AI will impact people of faith are already being asked. The answers vary widely, as you may well guess. Ellen Duffer writes in her work, "Religion & Politics":

"Religious communities have a significant stake in this conversation. Various faiths hold strong opinions regarding creation and the soul. As artificial intelligence moves forward, some researchers are engaging in thought experiments to prepare for the future, and to consider how current technology should be utilized by religious groups in the meantime" (Duffer, 2017).

When "Strong AI" becomes a reality and when androids themselves feel compelled by their reasoning to kneel down in prayer, will God answer? Such questions are already being asked, and for some, the answer is an emphatic "No" based on personhood. Others may not be so sure. Some observers say we should begin to regard super-intelligent robots as real persons (McGrath, 2011). Are you ready to do that?

The Ages of Man demarcate what one might call "quantum leaps" in progress. These historic "jumps" affected every aspect of how people lived and worked. Technology has changed our world in many ways, starting with pre-history and continuing through the present day.

The tight interconnectedness of all things technological, sociological, and even psychological, when associated with the near-term and prospective changes brought on by the convergence of Big Data, Artificial Intelligence, and Automation, is producing another "quantum leap" in how people will live, work, and perhaps consider their very humanity.

Quantum Leap! - Image courtesy of Pixabay

Consider faith and religion. The Godhead is already being revisited by the "Way of the Future" (WOTF) organization, according to Mark Harris, writing in Wired magazine, stating WOTF's activities include, but are not limited to:

". . . the realization, acceptance, and worship of a Godhead based on Artificial Intelligence (AI) developed through computer hardware and software" (Harris M., 2017).

I suspect that such a prospect will not likely be met with ambivalence, much less acceptance, by established fundamentalist Christian sects. AI as God is likely to be seen as not only blasphemous but outright heretical. Christian and Islamic fundamentalists share the same root belief concerning the Creator. They will not surrender their ideas easily to any artificial intelligence, no matter how "super" it might aspire to be or become (Charatan, 2018). Nor will the creation of an AI "church" likely change that prospect either now or later as we move deeper into the Age of Cognivity.

As if AI as God is not sufficiently shocking, thanks to discoveries brought by Big Data, Artificial Intelligence, and Automation, we may soon find ourselves asking, "What does it mean to be human?" Can we truly say we exercise free will when every aspect of our lives, all our wants, needs, fears, and desires, are subject to Big Data analysis and probable, if not certain, continuous manipulation? Can we be sure of anything? How can we be "certain" when the volume and velocity of data and the never-ending cascade of information on almost every possible matter and subject continues in constant flux and flow, overwhelming every sensibility? Will we not have to think differently and not so classically mechanical just to keep up? The answer is an emphatic yes! We may all be "Johnny Mnemonic" soon! (Acey, 2013)

The title, *The Age of Cognivity*, helps to better focus the reader's attention on the convergence of technologies like Big Data, Artificial Intelligence, and Automation and the impact on people, government, business, and society that is increasingly evident in our daily lives. Focusing one's attention is likely to be increasingly difficult under the circumstances but necessary.

Suppose we are to maximize the benefits of ever-accelerating advancements in information technologies, seemingly announced every day. In that case, we must first recognize the need for a shift in thinking to harness the methodologies, techniques, and procedures inherent in advanced analytics and frameworks.

For an excellent example, consider Activity-based Intelligence (ABI) analysis, broadly and from a multidisciplinary perspective. Typically, one or more analytical tools, or a methodology, would sit on top of information tools and technologies to assist analysts and researchers as they comb through and make sense of data's mounting volume and velocity. It would help analysts and researchers do it again in an iterative "wash, rinse, and repeat" fashion.

For instance, ABI specifically can be used in computer security and network defense with the understanding that such methods and techniques have universal application in the broader cyber analytics and information analysis domains.

The number of kinds and extent of cognitive bias is extensive, considered nearly a hundred or more by some counts (Yagoda, 2018). The question that remains unasked is whether technologies that may lead to digital enhancement, super-intelligent AI, and highly sophisticated robots will result in a "better" humanity? Or will we simply succumb more quickly and definitively to our already established personal prejudices and individual cognitive biases?

"Human beings are a disease, a cancer of this planet."

— *Agent Smith (Hugo Weaving), "The Matrix"*

Image courtesy of Pixabay (Altman, n.d.)

Warnings and cautions have already gone out for the need to beware of imposing our biases on the intelligent machines we are building. They may not be as forgiving, much less tolerant of human weakness, ignorance, and stupidity, as we biological entities often pretend to be. Agent Smith in the sci-fi cult film, *The Matrix*, could have many siblings who share his low opinion of Biological Humans. They may think we stink!

The victors always write history. It has been so since antiquity. Who are the victors now in this new age? They may be sentient, but will they be human? More importantly, what makes us all human? And if we are human, how can we survive as humans now and into the Age of Cognivity?

THE AGE OF COGNIVITY

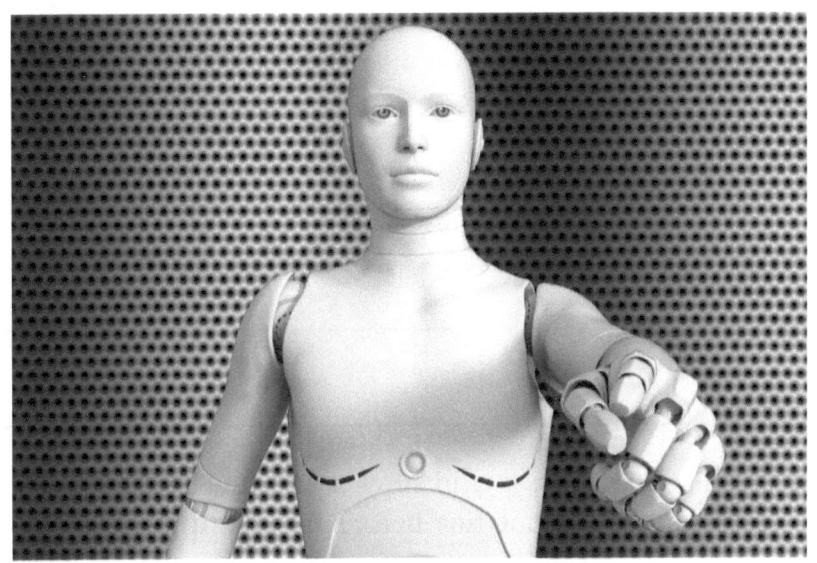

Image courtesy of Pixabay

CHAPTER 3 BIG DATA

"More data the better..."

What Big Data is and how it is transformative is crucial to understanding what lies before us heading into the Age of Cognivity.

Big Data - Image courtesy of Shutterstock

Datification of everything is well underway. As has been suggested, the term sounds ugly. Still, it means nothing more nor less than turning everything you can think of into data so it can be racked, stacked, and readied for manipulation to produce a better understanding of all facets of business, finance, politics, and government (Elliott, 2013).

Not surprisingly, for many, Big Data is whatever you want to call it. Be that as it may, here is a useful definition:

"Big data is data that exceeds the processing capacity of conventional database systems. The data is too big, moves too fast, or doesn't fit the strictures of your database architectures. To gain value from this data, you must choose an alternative way to process it" (Wilder-James, 2012). Imagine rivers of data flowing into oceans of more data, a rising tide of data, and you are far from the shore.

In other words, "Big Data" is simply more data than you can handle, but you must anyway.

Data Analytics - Image courtesy of Pixabay (Xresch, 2017)

While that may be a satisfactory definition, Big Data

carries some severe non-technical implications from a technical perspective. Data comes streaming, sometimes screaming, at us from every direction. We consume large amounts of information from the ubiquitous, 24/7, All News cable channels like CNN, MSNBC, and Fox News, to name a few. Increasingly, we are turning to social media outlets for both news and information (Nations, 2018). The most popular are the usual suspects: Facebook, Reddit, and Twitter (Kallas, 2018). The list is likely to grow and change as we drive ever headlong and deeper into the Age of Cognivity!

Big Data means different things to different people based on circumstance and purpose. One could develop many different definitions, and not all would be entirely satisfactory in every circumstance (Press, 2014). That should not surprise anyone, considering the current wide application of the term.

Resorting to the basic Merriam-Webster definition of Big Data as "an accumulation of data that is too large and complex for processing by traditional management tools," while not particularly inspiring, does work (Merriam Webster, 2018). We can, however, expand on the definition, as is done in Wikipedia:

"Current usage of the term 'big data' tends to refer to predictive analytics, user behavior analytics, or certain other advanced data analysis methods that extract value from data, and seldom to a particular size of data set" (Wikipedia, 2018).

The expansion is much closer to what we like to think about when discussing Big Data and its potential impacts on business, government, and society. Development happens principally through discovery since, by definition, the volume, velocity, and variety of data make Big Data so "large and challenging to manage, much less to make any sense of quickly and efficiently. Volume readily speaks for itself. Velocity is about how fast the data comes in or goes out. Variety is suggestive of how many kinds of data require processing. (Gewirtz, 2018) Application of technology to deal with Big Data includes, but is not limited to, Artificial Intelligence (AI) and Automation making advanced analytics possible.

More purposefully, data volume is composed of several elements. Each affects the other to make Big Data what it is, not only in size but in shape. Each part has its requirements.

The elements include:

Collection

The collection of new data, such as a sensor that collects 12 megabytes of data per hour.

Transfer

Transfer of data, such as a network of weather sensors that transfers 64 terabytes of data to servers each month.

Processing

Data processing includes a settlement process at a bank that processes eight terabytes of data each morning.

Storage

Data sits in storage, such as an organization with 124 databases that collectively hold 77 petabytes of data (Spacey, 2017).

While "quantity" can have a special quality of its own, especially when it comes to data, so can velocity, described here as such:

"Data velocity is the speed at which data is processed. This includes input, such as processing social media posts, and output, such as the processing required to produce a report or execute a process" (Spacey, 2017).

Thinking about the data

Not to be too overwhelmed, making sense of it all requires adjustment and a new way of thinking about data. Hence, a new paradigm for the Cognitive Age that goes far beyond what characterized Ages before. One very real world example requiring a shift in thinking about data and what we think we know is taking place right now in the area of National Security, Intelligence, and Defensive Cyber Operations, specifically, Activity-based Intelligence (ABI) analysis and Object-based production (OBP).

Image courtesy of Pixabay (Linforth, Hacker, n.d.)

Activity-based intelligence (ABI) analysts are deeply immersed in Big Data, as are other analysts inside and outside of government. For ABI, analysts engaged in the Cyber Fight, Transactions, Activity, and Correlations (TAC) dominate. Former National Geospatial-Intelligence Agent (NGA) Letitia Long defines Activity Based Intelligence as "a discipline of intelligence where the analysis and subsequent collection focus on the activity and transactions associated with an entity, a population or an area of interest." Furthermore, she says expressly, "These activities and transactions are not solely tied to geospatial actions, but also apply across the cyber, social, financial, and commercial domains" (Long, 2013). Indeed, for ABI analysts working on cyber incidents, TAC is very special and informative for discovery.

What do I mean by all that? For instance, when users communicate over the Internet, they engage in a "transaction" in the classic sense of ABI. One can argue that the "three-way-handshake" is a "transaction" between TC/IP devices. The "activity" occurs according to communication protocols, the "rules" of the transaction, and the OSI model's standardization of communication functions. Communication happens because of protocols followed, transactions initiated, data flows, and activity terminated according to the same rules. And everything happens at the speed of cyber. The ABI analyst's task is to detect, identify, and sort through those transactions and correlate them in a way that makes sense in producing actionable intelligence. ABI's "Four Pillars" provide the foundation for doing precisely that.

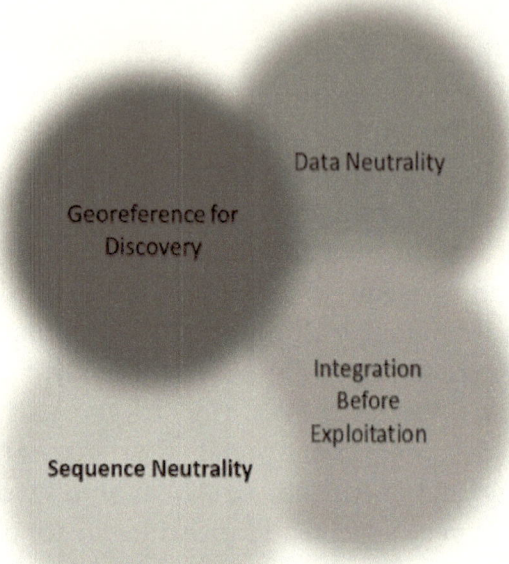

Fig. 1 The "Four Pillars" of ABI (SOURCE: Various)

Intelligence analysts trained in ABI methodology are familiar with the terms "geo-registration for discovery," "data neutrality," "sequence neutrality," and "integration before exploitation," as explained in great detail and with considerable clarity in Patrick Biltgen and Stephan Ryan's extensively referenced book, *Activity Based Intelligence: Principles and Applications*, available from Amazon (Biltgen & Ryan, 2016). Transactions, activity, and correlations are all given extensive treatment. For the ABI analyst in the cyber arena, the "Four Pillars" open up the space for wider-ranging analysis and offer the prospect of identifying and even discovering "unknown unknowns" that may have significant consequences through an investigation or an offensive or defensive cyber campaign.

Cyberspace is a virtual world that resides within the

physical world. NSA Director Adm. Michael Rogers has remarked, "Every single component has a physical geographic position on the face of the Earth." Dual-hatted as commander of U.S. Cyber Command at the time, Rogers said it was not enough to throw down a network schematic on a conference table but rather, "... show me where it is because there are lots of ways to try to understand things" (USGIF, 2015). That was why Rogers called for a closer relationship between the National Security Agency (NSA) and the National Geospatial-Intelligence Agency (NGA). The "lots of ways" Adm. Rogers suggests is precisely what ABI is all about —even for cyber, it is not just log and security file analysis, PCAP traces, and vulnerability reports.

Geolocation also matters in cyberspace; however, data must be correlated from multi-INT, All Source Intelligence to be of optimal value.

"Multi-INT" refers to the fusion or correlation of different data types into a complete picture. The data can come from public sources, often referenced as Open Source Intelligence (OSINT). OSINT can include unstructured information from chat feeds and social media websites like Twitter and Facebook. The objective is to provide the most complete and intelligent picture possible to support informed decisions (Harris Corporation, n.d.).

The sourcing requirement is all and more. The All-Source Intelligence need is one of the precursors of the Age of Cognivity.

Chandler P. Atwood describes ABI's multi-INT approach to data as "transformational" in both impact and scope (Atwood, 2015). Since ABI takes a multi-INT, all-source approach to data collection, processing, and interpretation, analysts can build upon all "Four Pillars" of ABI to solve CYBINT and Counter-CYBINT problems. The interplay of transactions, activity, and correlations form a mosaic revealing the who, what, and why of suspicious computer network activity and malicious cyber campaigns.

At the center of ABI is a correlation concerning integration before exploitation, one of the "Four Pillars" of ABI (Biltgen & Ryan, 2016, pp. 255-256). In fact, in their book on ABI, Biltgen and Ryan spend an entire chapter on correlation and data fusion. Both art and science are evident and intricately bound up in making the kind of associations, correlations, and relationships from data collected that lead to estimations and assessments in intelligence analysis.

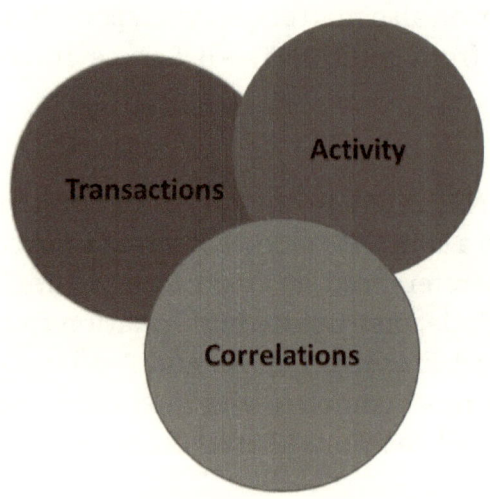

Fig. 2 TAC Relations and ABI (SOURCE: Various)

Transactions, activity, and correlations (TAC) are BIG drivers of ABI investigations and analysis. Correlation is the key to understanding computer network activity as well. That same kind of shift in thinking very much informs and enhances the "sense-making" required when dealing with Big Data, leveraged by

Artificial Intelligence and Automation characteristics of "applied" Cognivity.

Because ABI is all-source and multi-INT, cyber investigators benefit at multiple levels, including, but not limited to, the physical network layer, the logical layer, and the cyber human persona layer—when it comes to countering targeted threat activity (DoD, 2013).

ABI, however, does not exist in analytical isolation. Object-based production (OBP) is significantly enhanced when combined with ABI techniques and methods. According to Charlotte Shabarekh, the former head of Analytics, Modeling, and Simulation at Aptiva, Inc., now at the MIT's Lincoln Lab,"In Cyber, OBP is a challenging task due to spoofing or masking of IP addresses. It's necessary to perform 'co-reference resolution' tasks to associate spoofed packets to the correct source address" (Shabarekh, 2016).

ABI can provide the required context to accurately perform the necessary data associations in cyber network defense operations.

Again, that does not exclude other methodologies. Whether it is the "Diamond Model" or the "Cyber Kill-Chain," an ABI analyst has access to all information sources and the means to prosecute investigations and make threat assessments. Doing so is a core concept in understanding activity-based intelligence (ABI) in the cyber domain.

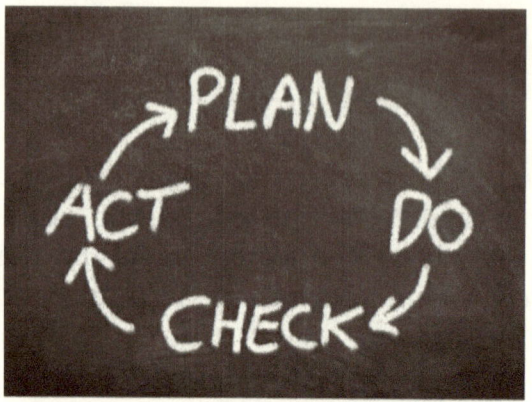

Image courtesy of Pixabay (Linforth, Plan, Do, Check, Act Loop, n.d.)

All these models and methodologies continue to evolve and benefit from the convergence of advanced technologies associated with Big Data, Artificial Intelligence, and Automation as the Age of Cognivity takes a firm, if not dominating, hold. While ABI application is seen most predominantly in the arena of National Security and Defensive Cyber Analysis, the same kind of holistic, "quantum" shift in thinking and knowing that makes ABI work currently is what will work and characterize much of what we will see manifest in the Age of Cognivity.

As difficult as it may be to imagine, there was a time when if you wanted the benefit of Big Data Analytics, you had to "roll your own," as it were, using Hadoop, the open-source software of choice for building Big Data platforms. Having to do it yourself is no longer the case. There are dozens, if not more than a hundred, vendors who can accommodate a commercial client's needs, either on-premises or in the Cloud. The market for big data hit $166 billion in 2018, and according to some researchers, it is only likely to grow to as much as $266 billion worldwide by 2022 (Whiting, 2019).

As in the commercial sector, big is beautiful, and Big Government "owns" Big Data in the public sector. The Department of Defense (DOD) owns a lot of Big Data, considering the need to protect global communications networks. The Defense Information Systems Agency (DISA) is very keen to operate expansively in the Cloud globally (Mitchell, 2018). DISA's Cyber Situational Awareness Analytical Capabilities (CSAAC) platform is crucial to DOD's mission to protect Department of Defense information networks (DODIN), systems, and most sensitive data.

According to DISA, CSAAC provides the following types of capability:

DODIN operations and situational awareness. Monitoring of DOD Enterprise Email is an example of CSAAC providing operators with near real-time situational awareness on incidents, detailed provisioning statuses, email gateway filtering, and more.

Defensive cyber operations (DCO). Fight by Indicator (FbI) is an example of a defensive cyber operations capability within CSAAC. FbI provides enterprise computer network defense analysts with the ability to automate workflows that review cyber threat reports and extract potential indicators and warnings for further processing and, if needed, execution of an automated DOD countermeasures workflow.

Anomaly detection. The anomaly detection suite is a CSAAC capability focused on detecting authorized users who pose a threat to the confidentiality, integrity, or availability of sensitive DOD data. The service also allows analysts to alert the proper authorities if a potential insider threat is detected (Department of Defense, 2016).

When you look closely, you can see CSAAC is doing quite a bit more than just storing data for ease of retrieval. CSAAC is a proven technology and a template for BD integration within the Data Analytics Domain. The combination of CSSAC and BD enhances workflow. It provides considerable "reach-back" to confirm further findings supporting decisions at the strategic, operational, and tactical levels of cybersecurity and defensive cyber operations (DCO).

Both ABI and OBP facilitate analysis when sitting above BD platforms like CSAAC. The Law of Accelerating Returns, converging technologies, and advanced quantum computational capabilities force information consumers and users to engage their thinking in new ways (Kurzweil R. , 2005), all of which are required to get the most benefit from the quantum-level changes characterizing how we all will live, know, and do.

Lastly, for inference, intended or otherwise, think *Minority Report* without Pre-Cogs. This works very well, perhaps too well for some people's liking.

Another good example is AURORA by CENTCOMGLOBAL, which delves into AI and human behavior. According to the vendor, the implications are without limit:

"The applications of AURORA are not solely rooted in the intelligence community. Multiple versions of the algorithm can be applied for commercial application to study consumer intent, or to other government agencies to reduce fraud, waste, and abuse, in the healthcare industry for medical records and patient information, pharmaceuticals and new drug development, or in universities and research centers to assist with pattern analysis of advanced sciences and theoretical physics. As the world becomes more connected and the advancement of technology increases, the applications for AURORA become limitless" (CENTCOM Global, 2017).

Speaking of applications, particularly in the United States, we have yet to come to any kind of consensus on when precisely the authorities, armed with the findings of Big Data, Artificial Intelligence, and Automation, should intervene, despite the number and significance of "red flags" and associative alarms (Kassner, 2019).

Inference - Image courtesy of Pixabay (Ide, n.d.)

The convergence of Big Data, Artificial Intelligence, and Automation, not necessarily in any order, may influence the debate, but not likely seriously. At least not until the consequences of not applying lessons learned to permit law enforcement to intervene sooner than current laws allow becomes genuinely compelling. The Age of Cognivity is upon us. Some aspects of the new Age are likely to prove uncomfortable both ethically and constitutionally.

The science and technologies associated with Big Data Analytics are exciting and continue growing in capability and implementation. Data science projects for business, government, and non-government agencies are seemingly limitless in number and scope. They are restrained only by the imaginations and creativity of data scientists and data engineers. Privacy concerns are likely also to grow exponentially.

The Age of Cognition is an age that is characterized by the use of information and communication technologies to improve knowledge acquisition and dissemination. It is an era where humans can access vast amounts of information at their fingertips. In addition to these technological advances, we see a shift in the way people think about themselves and their surroundings.

CHAPTER 4 ARTIFICIAL INTELLIGENCE

"The excitement is real ..."

Artificial Intelligence (AI) is no longer the buzzword it once was, reserved for computer literate elites and computer software vendors selling the next "Big Thing" in computer applications.

Artificial Intelligence is proving itself in business, finance, science, and engineering. According to Richard Gray:, writing for the BBC:

"We stand on the edge of a crucial moment in the history of our species – a time when the creation of our own inventiveness has the potential to change everything. For some, it will be humanity's salvation, while for others, it could be our downfall. We are entering the age of artificial intelligence (AI)" (Gray, 2018).

The connection between Big Data and AI should be obvious. In many cases, it is AI to the rescue when it comes to mounds of data (Walach, 2019). However, not all is rosy in the Wondrous World of AI.

I am Not Artificial - Image courtesy of Pixabay (Altmann, Robot Human Machine, n.d.)

The idea that AI inevitably benefits liberal democracies the most is questionable, with some concern that authoritarian regimes like Russia and China, instead, have already demonstrated that they have the advantage in AI and are using that advantage to coercive effect (Thompson & Bremmer, 2018). Thanks to the leveraging effect AI has regarding Big Data, enhanced by automation, the challenges to liberal democracies will be increasingly significant in the Cognitive Age (Nuwer, 2017).

A simple definition of Artificial Intelligence is getting machines to act like humans. An argument could be made, "Why would anyone want to do that?" And "Getting humans to act like humans is difficult and has been for centuries." Nice! After all, wouldn't we want intelligence machines to act "smarter" than people instead of seeking to emulate the lowest common denominator? Of course, and even with that said, getting there has been challenging. Daniel Newman, a contributor to *Forbes*, makes the point that thanks to Big Data, AI is now flat-out a necessity for government, business, and arguably even for individuals:

"With the steady growth of data produced by the Internet of Things (IoT), businesses will be turning to machine learning to process, trend, and analyze the information. Indeed, machine learning AI isn't just a nice-to-have in 2018; it's a must-have. It's the only way companies can make valuable sense of the flow of data—both structured and unstructured—coming in" (Newman, 2017).

What goes into and comes out of computers, much less advanced AI, is getting much closer scrutiny. AI is only as good as the algorithms involved (Asay, 2016). That is another way of saying, "Stupidity in! Stupidity out!" Of course, what, then, if the algorithms are wrong? Considering that humans create algorithms, at least mostly right now, algorithms designed may very well be just as contaminated by their creators' same biases and prejudices.

Few could argue that AI has not taken a tight hold in business, particularly, if not especially, when trying to figure out the return on investment, or ROI, in various circumstances. What remains the long pole in the data "tent" is getting a grip on Big Data in the first place so that AI can chew on it. Collection, where one must turn to some sort of automation to make everything come out reasonably well, not just to clean up the data but organize both structured and unstructured for a useful purpose. Process automation, customer engagement, and data insights seem to be the biggest payoffs producing the quickest wins (Davenport & Ronanki, 2018).

Increasingly familiar are the effects of "narrow" AI. Examples abound, but more on that in a moment. Indeed, people are taking AI very seriously on many levels, including, but not limited to, moral and ethical considerations. In its 2018 annual report, the AI Now Institute raises the question, "Who is responsible when AI systems harm us?" The report answers the question by recommending accountability measures to provide governance of such powerful technologies (The AI Now Institute, 2018). The question is deceptive on many levels. It raises more questions than it answers. Is the government going to regulate AI research and application? Is that a good thing when the government is a primary abuser of such technologies? What does a court of law do when a robot kills or injures a biological human? Terminate the robot, or sue its makers? Perhaps both. What then does AI compliance look like from a regulatory perspective? These compelling questions will likely shape much of the legal environment in the Age of Cognivity.

When most people think of AI, they think of robots. But, one must think of AI in three different ways. One could say AI comes in at least three flavors. They are Narrow, General, and Super AI. Thinking of AI narrowly, in Artificial Narrow Intelligence (ANI) terms, you can say that is what we see already concerning handling and serving up AI the way Google does now (Traugott, 2017). General AI, or Artificial General Intelligence (AGI), is more exciting and fits most people's science-fiction notion of a robot: a machine that thinks like the average biological human (Heath, 2018). You could say HAL 9000 from the 1968 science fiction film, *2001: A Space Odyssey*, is a prime example. An AGI that decides biological humans are a threat to our own or their existence might be more concerning. Now that is a gnarly thought (Harris S., 2015). Super AI, or Superintelligent AI, breaks all bounds. Super AI or Artificial Super Intelligence (ASI) is very much Post-Singularity, if you can imagine that; most people cannot.

A new generation of AI tools is taking the world by storm. Among the most popular is ChatGPT. ChatGPT is a chatbot that was first released by OpenAI in November of 2022. ChatGPT is designed to respond with human-like text when prompted (Fedewa, 2023). The popular response has been overwhelming. Within just a couple months, ChatGPT was estimated to have a 100 million users, much to the notice of not just big business, but lawmakers as well (Bartz, 2023). Suddenly, everyone, it seemed, want to get hands-on with ChatGPT.

Interestingly, ChatGPT had this to say about "Cognivity":

"It sounds like 'cognivity' is being used to describe a state of being that involves being aware of and taking advantage of the benefits of technology, specifically in the areas of big data, artificial intelligence, and automation. It could be interpreted as a way of describing how someone is able to use these technologies to improve their knowledge and thinking, and to be more effective in their work and life. Essentially, it is about being able to use technology in a way that enhances one's cognitive abilities and capabilities."

An excellent assessment. Surprisingly well-thought, it would appear, coming from an AI. I may be biased, however.

ChatGPT has been praised and condemned as a harbinger of things to come. Doomsayers predict ChatGPT will take your job. ChatGPT will turn on you. ChatGPT will take your girlfriend! This is just speculation to be sure, especially the last bit, but you get the gist of the discussion. I suspect some may be happy if ChatGPT takes their job (Rainie & Anderson, 2023), especially if by mastering ChatGPT they get their work done quicker and better, and then maybe even get promoted!

ChatGPT is just the beginning. Technology Labs everywhere are humming with research activity (Bean, 2023) (Naysmith, 2023). ChatGPT, itself, still needs human input and prompts to do its magic, but that may not necessarily be the case with other, more advanced Generative AI in the future. The progress is happening that fast.

So where is all this going? Sam Altman, the CEO of OpenAI, says, "Artificial General Intelligence (AGI) is the single most important and transformative technology that will ever be created in human history" (Ordonez, Dunn, & Noll, 2023). He may be exaggerating, but perhaps not by much.

So what do we mean by "Generative AI" in the first place? Well, according to London journalist, George Lawton, writing for TechTarget:

"Generative AI is a type of artificial intelligence technology that can produce various types of content including text, imagery, audio and synthetic data" (Lawton, 2023).

This is simple enough. It seems hardly worth all the buzz, but it is indeed transformative in its own right.

Meanwhile, use of other AI tools like DALL-E 2.0, designed to create images from text, and Steve.ai, by Animaker, which allows the user to easily create high-quality videos, are generating significant interest, as well as Copy.ai for writers and content creators. All are becoming widely accepted and used (Rebelo, 2023) (Raghaven, 2023).

There are hundreds more AI applications, including many AI platforms, ranging from TensorFlow to Watson to Google, being used and improved upon (Kenyon, 2021). The deluge continues as AI becomes increasingly ubiquitous at home, at work, and in school. The saying, "There's an app for that," is rapidly becoming, "There's an AI app for that!" There's more to come as we dive ever deeper into the Age of Cognivity!

The real and potential risks of AI, meanwhile, are not being ignored, nor minimized. The dangers are receiving serious consideration by technologists, from educators, and the government. The National Institute of Standards and Technology (NIST) is keeping close track. NIST has released an Artificial Intelligence Risk Management Frame Work 1.0 (RMF 1.0), the purpose of which is to provide guidance to public and private entities as they go about assessing and managing AI Systems (Bryan & Fath, 2023). The NIST publication focuses on the tough questions about the risks involved in creating and managing AI systems. RMF 1.0 offers guidance on the risks, impacts, and harm potentially posed by AI systems. Also considered are the many challenges involved in managing AI systems and networks. RMF 1.0 emphasizes this fundamental point:

"Risk management should be continuous, timely, and performed throughout the AI system
lifecycle dimensions" (Locascio, 2023).

Now, as we stand just within the bounds of the outer perimeter of the Age of Cognivity, the danger signs from AI can be seen, at least dimly. Observers are saying out loud, "Truth is dead!" Matthew Wall, writing for the BBC, adds:

"AI could be a powerful force for good, improving healthcare and combating climate change, for example. But it also presents many dangers—to democracy, to financial markets, to the belief in objective truth. Data in the wrong hands, used in the wrong way, could even threaten world peace, some commentators warn" (Wall, 2019).

Matthew Wall is not alone in his assessment. Understanding why we succumb to false beliefs is crucial in protecting ourselves and our Republic from manipulation. The problem is no longer not having enough data upon which to base decisions but rather not knowing where the information comes from and the underlying context considering the ever-increasing reliance on social media sources (O'Connor & Weatherall, 2019). Again, AI, in the wrong hands, can be used to misinform, mislead, and manipulate the public to not just general mischief, but to violence and insurrection.

Alarms have been raised about the use of AI to generate and spread misinformation and disinformation. The problem is well and above the usual propaganda of governments and their intelligence agencies. Profit-focused news and information outlets can also succumb, as well as political operators too. A Georgetown University Center for Security and Emerging Technology Report contends, in detail:

"For malicious actors looking to spread propaganda—information designed to shape
perceptions to further an actor's interest—these language models bring the promise of automating the
creation of convincing and misleading text for use in influence operations, rather than having to rely on human labor. For society, these developments bring a new set of concerns: the prospect of highly
scalable—and perhaps even highly persuasive—campaigns by those seeking to covertly influence public
opinion" (Goldstein, et al., 2023).

Data is everywhere – Image courtesy of Shutterstock

There is a growing amount of literature that further supports the case that AI, even uncomplicated Generative Language Models, can do great harm in the hands of those who mean to do so. The danger comes from such models being used offensively for malicious purposes and deception (Booth, 2016). This is a a danger that is not likely to go away as Large Language Models improve and become more capable. Those improvements may include more Big Data and even Self-learning (Toews, 2023). Yet another indicator that we are indeed diving ever deeper into the "Age of Cognivity!"

How often have you heard someone say, "Just connect the dots!" All very nice! But first, you must "collect" the dots and store them somewhere. You must evaluate the dots for relevance, timeliness, and influential relationships before trying to make sense of it all: Big Data, Artificial Intelligence, and Automation to the rescue.

Connections – Image courtesy of Pixabay (Barta, n.d.)

Based on what we know about Quantum Cognition, at least in the popular mind, thinking in quantum terms helps to complete the picture connecting the dots, or at least revealing the connections. Yearsley and Busemeyer have both written well separately and together on Quantum Cognition (Yearsley & Busemeyer, 2015). The reader should seek them out. They need no correction nor amplification from me. I champion their insights and contributions. Their peer-reviewed formal work on quantum models for decision-making has been extensively peer-reviewed and well-received.

CHAPTER 5
AUTOMATION

"I want it automatically..."

Automation, while not new, takes on even greater importance with the challenge posed by ever-growing amounts of data, the proliferation of Big Data platforms, and the AI needed to use specified content. Ironically, even today, information specialists and intelligence analysts spend extensive time identifying and collecting data, then processing the data into a form that can be analyzed to produce actionable intelligence for either business or government.

Artificial Intelligence and Automation touch nearly every aspect of human life or nearly so. J. Bloom, a business correspondent writing for the BBC, makes this clear:

"Automation is not just about robots or self-driving cars, it can also involve computer programs and algorithms, but the message from this analysis is clear: the better trained and educated you are, the lower are the chances of you losing your job" (Bloom, 2019).

Surprisingly, even today, much of the work for those doing

research is painstakingly manual and time-consuming. The onset of Big Data Platforms (BDP) and AI only adds to the problem of making sense of it all. That is where Automation with a capital "A" comes into play. Collection is often the first step in tackling an intractable problem. What do we know? Where is the data? How do we access the data? Automation can address those questions and more.

How, where, and sometimes, determining how much automation is needed to achieve a business or national security intelligence objective is complex. How Big Data Platforms integrate Artificial Intelligence and Automation into their features will be exciting as the drive forward into the Age of Cognivity accelerates. If automation does away with 47 percent of the jobs in America by 2030, we may see changes like never before and a cultural shift that would be the challenge of the age (Frey & Osborne, 2013). What am I talking about? Universal Basic Income! Now there's a thought!

Job losses are continually being blamed on automation amplified by AI. Estimates run in hundreds of millions of jobs, if not billions, lost, globally, in the decades ahead (Kolmer, 2023). And those are not the most pessimistic estimates. This is worrisome, to say the least.

By now, it should be clear that retraining will be necessary in the face of such losses. Unfortunately, not everyone will be happy at the prospect, especially if it means the end of the life they used to have (Margolis, 2016). For many people, change is hard. Suppose heavy manufacturing is all one knows and has experienced. In that case, retraining for a non-manufacturing job that raises the prospect of forcing one out of a comfortable working class position may be difficult to accept. Regardless, that may very well be one result of the expansion of automation that favors a "knowledge" economy. According to the McKinsey Institute, Advanced Robotics is one of the technologies that will ". . . have the potential to disrupt the status quo, alter the way people live and work . . ." (Manyika, et al., 2013). That may turn out to be an understatement.

Low-skill jobs that are primarily routine, repetitive, simple, or physical are the most likely Automation and AI augmentation targets. According to the research, that could put 52 million American jobs at risk by the year 2030, including such positions as ". . . office administration, production, transportation, and food preparation" (Sherman, 2019). Mappings of where automation will displace the most workers indicated mid-level jobs would take the brunt of the changes in the AI era, particularly in smaller towns and rural areas of America (Misra, 2019). Although automation is not a new phenomenon in human history, this time, blue-collar workers are not the only ones who will be seriously affected. Again, from Richard Gray, writing for the BBC's Future Now project:

"Often, we think of low-wage, low-skill jobs being the most at risk, like warehouse workers or cashiers, but automation may also affect middle-income jobs, such as clerks, chefs, office workers, security guards, junior lawyers, and inspectors" (Gray, 2017).

Not surprisingly, with so many women in the workforce, automation is likely to have severe gender-based implications. The data already show more than a potential trend, but a seriously sustained, long-term impact extending well into the Age of Cognivity. According to Sarah Holder who writes in CITYLAB:

"While women make up only half of the labor force,

researchers found that they make up 58 percent of the workers at the highest risk of automation. Among them, Hispanic women could be most affected due to the professions where they're most highly concentrated. Meanwhile, the share of women working as computer scientists and systems analysts, software developers, and computer support specialists has declined since 2000, leaving the task of shaping the proverbial Future of Work mostly to men" (Holder, 2019).

Change is coming, however. Women are gaining political prominence at both the national and local levels. The issue will increasingly be reflected in the results of political election campaigns, stressing the number of jobs and the quality of the positions involved for women.

The challenge, naturally, will be in retraining, up-skilling, and perhaps the relocation of workers. Remote work too. Also, cognitive skill upgrades may be necessary to fill jobs untouched and created by Artificial Intelligence and Automation.

The colossal task of re-skilling is likely to fall on governments. The cost would be too prohibitive for business, with estimates running in the tens of billions of dollars (LeVine, 2019). Also, the assumption that those needing re-skilling will jump at the opportunity may not be as well-founded as one might think. There will be those who will not be able to make the transition or refuse to do so. The reasons may have little to do with economic status or education. The difference may have everything to do with how one thinks and develops a metacognitive response to change. The pushback may be cultural and even gender-dependent. There will be those who will find making the transition extremely difficult for various psychosocial factors.

How will those more comfortable relying on their "native wit" and immediate, instinctive, "gut response" fare in the Age of Cognivity? Will they be able to eventually, given enough time, acquire the job skills that will be increasingly in demand, or will they be added to the growing ranks of the "Permanent Dependent Class" and become the primary recipients of Universal Basic Income (UBI) (Diamandis, 2016)? They very well might, for a variety of reasons. According to Futurist Ray Kurzweil, the time is coming sooner rather than later:

"In the early 2030s, we'll have universal basic income in the developed world, and worldwide by the end of the 2030s. You'll be able to live very well on that" (Schwartz, 2018).

What is worse is the data shows job losses over the next five years are not likely to be limited to low-paid jobs, not only in the United States but other developed countries, according to Jane Gilmore, writing about the Fourth Industrial Revolution:

"Around 40% of Australia's medical practitioners are women, but they are dramatically under-represented in positions of seniority and areas of high specialty and ground-breaking research. As with fast-food workers, this makes female doctors vulnerable to job losses due to automation" (Gilmore, 2016).

The fear of automation is real and only likely to grow as automation, supplemented with artificial intelligence, takes a firm grip on the employment marketplace, or as some might say, a stranglehold, if all the negatives prove out, as has been already suggested by the press and politicians (Banas, 2019). Although some progress is already being made in implementing UBI, the main issue may revolve around its politics. According to some commentators, both the political left and the political right have laid claims to UBI to foster the utopian dream of "paying people just to be alive" or as a ploy to gut the welfare state (Battiston, 2017). Regardless of how the political winds end up blowing, UBI will be a significant factor in the Age of Cognivity. Politicians like Andrew Yang are already making UBI a vital issue in their bids for political power. He says one in three Americans risk losing their jobs to technologies like big data, artificial intelligence, and automation. Press reports describe Yang's plan as:

"A form of universal basic income, Yang's so-called 'Freedom Dividend' is the centerpiece of his campaign. He says it would end poverty in the 'most direct manner possible,' support those whose lives have been disrupted by AI and automation, and share the prosperity the new economy has created (and thus far distributed unevenly)" (DeCosta-Klipa , 2019).

What then about the nature of work, one might ask? If UBI becomes the norm, what will it mean to work? The notion that you have to go somewhere to do work will vanish. The very idea of commuting to work will change. In fact, in a knowledge economy, commuting is wasteful. One could argue that commuting will still be necessary for some workers. Firefighters, law enforcement, and corrections officers will still have to go to a place where work will be conducted.

The pandemic of 2020 was just a foreshadowing of what to expect. Millions of workers found they could do their jobs remotely. Technology platforms such as Zoom helped workers to collaborate and coordinate work. After the worst of the pandemic, some workers refused to return to the office.

Many companies are looking at ways to help employees continue working remotely while still keeping them productive. Some companies are offering flexible hours, remote work options, and even paid time off (Chen & Fulmer, 2018). Others are providing access to online tools like Zoom and Slack.

Even in an environment where robots will be frequently encountered, they will not always be everywhere. Biological humans will still be needed to do the work even after the coming Singularity. Deloitte, among other employers, have been looking into the complicated dynamics of an augmented workforce and how that savages our traditional thinking about the nature of work (Schartz, Walsh, Collins, Stockton, & Wagner, 2017). Does the question then become how does a biological human feel about suddenly becoming an "augmentee" in the Age of Cognivity?

According to a World Bank 2019 assessment: "Technology is changing the skills that employers seek. Workers need to be better at complex problem-solving, teamwork, and adaptability" (World Bank, 2019).

Complex problem-solving skills will be at a premium before, during, and after the coming Singularity, being especially critical when biological humans must compete with super-intelligent robots and advanced AI. We like to think there are some things human beings can do better than machines. That idea is already being tested to the limit. What then does this all mean for you? According to Carol Stubbings at Price Waterhouse:

"As individuals – actual human beings – what do we need to do to thrive and prosper in whatever the new world brings? The secret for a bright future seems to me to lie in flexibility and in the ability to reinvent yourself. If you believe that the future lies in STEM skills and that interests you, train for that. But be prepared to rethink if the world does not need so many programmers. If you are a great accountant who has prospered by building strong client relationships, think about how you can apply that capability, without necessarily having to be an accountant. Think about yourself as a bundle of skills and capabilities, not a defined role or profession" (Stubbings, 2018).

Of course, most people say, "That all sounds good, but what do I do now?" Some people will have great difficulty thinking of themselves as a "bundle of skills," mainly if they have seen themselves as steelworkers and union men and women all their lives. They have a history of going down to the plant in town, punching in, and standing on the assembly line, pulling the lever that mashes out widgets eight hours a day. Any shift in thinking is very likely to collide with issues of identity and self-respect that will be hard to overcome.

The loss of jobs due to automation remains a significant concern. However, it's not the sole concern. Automated attacks coming through cyberspace are no longer science fiction. According to Larry Johnson, the problem is just beginning:

"Malwarebytes, Symantec and McAfee all predicted that AI-based cyber-attacks would emerge in 2019, and become more and more of a significant threat in the next few years.

"What this means is that we are on the verge of a new age in cybersecurity, where hackers will be able to unleash formidable new attacks using self-directed software tools and processes" (Johnson L. , 2018).

As we head not only further into the Age of Cognivity, the question of what needs to be done to protect ourselves and our information is growing. Reports abound, and considerable thinking as to what needs to be done is flourishing. Bret Piatt, a cybersecurity CEO writing in Forbes, says more clearly:

"Protecting your data today means dealing with hacking attempts powered by machine learning (ML), the science of computers learning and acting like humans. These ML computer algorithms are based on an analytical model designed to collect data and adapt its processes and activities according to use and experience, getting 'smarter' over time" (Piatt, 2018).

Some might say, "Hmm! Protecting our robot friends? That sounds like a job for me!" Basically, yes. Ironically, what biological humans may find themselves doing as the Age of Cognivity settles in may have us tending to the machines rather than the other way around! What about creativity, innovation, and emotional support?

Then again, maybe not. In fact, you might find yourself sitting down with your boss, and he says:

"I need you, Deck. This is a bad one, the worst yet. I need the old Blade Runner; I need your magic" (Blade Runner Quotes. (n.d), 2019).

The quote is from the Ridley Scott film, *Blade Runner*, with its all-star cast of Harrison Ford, Rutger Hauer, Sean Young, Edward James Olmos, and M. Emmet Walsh. The film needs no introduction to the reader, I am sure, but the irony of it all is compelling when discussing super-intelligent robots, or, in this case, so-called Replicants. Who among us would really want Deckard's job?

Biological humans to the rescue. Patrick Coleman, in an opinion piece on "Fatherly," a parenting site for men, says that despite all expectations in the '70s and '80s, our education system is still geared to churning out factory workers:

"No one saw Bill Gates coming. But everyone sees Mark Zuckerberg, and most of us seem to understand that the disruptors of the future are already on their way. Still, public school curriculums are built around soon-to-be-outdated technological lessons rather than around the sorts of soft skills needed to find human employment in a robotic age" (Coleman, 2019).

Soft skills versus science, technology, engineering, and math sound like a poor matchup, but perhaps not as much as one may think. We must think for ourselves, and so will our children and grandchildren. While we may not be able to fully "robot-proof" ourselves, putting concerns and emphasis back where they need to be will be crucial for the future of ourselves, our children, and humankind (Eisikovits & Feldman, 2019), not just concerning propositional knowledge but far into deeper realms of human thinking, focusing holistically, creatively, and in full-spectrum cognitive mode!

The Metaverse

As if all this was not enough, there is also the prospect of the Metaverse. How will we live, work, and play in the Metaverse? We are already beginning to get an idea.

THE AGE OF COGNIVITY

I can see it - Image by Riki32 from Pixabay

The Metaverse comprises virtual worlds where billions of people can interact from anywhere in the world on their computers (Ravenscroft, 2022). There is much more to the Metaverse than that, as described, even now, in the Encyclopedia Britannica:

"**Metaverse**: proposed network of immersive online worlds experienced typically through virtual reality or augmented reality in which users would interact with each other and purchase goods and services, some of which would exist only in the online world" (Gregersen, (n.d)).

How about Zoom on steroids in 3D? Or virtual reality games, too? Or maybe a reimagining of "Tranquility Lane" from Fallout 3, but "re-realized" as a persistent virtual world with virtual concerts and entertainment? There will be something for everyone.

Why is this happening now, one might ask? Because we are deep in a universe dominated by quantum change, continuously being blasted by the Law of Accelerating Returns, big data, artificial intelligence, and automation.

CHAPTER 6 THINKING

"I am thinking, deeply..."

When it comes to thinking, most people will usually tell you what they think. Or at least what they want you to believe they are thinking! Friends, family, and co-workers often have little difficulty telling you what they think, regardless of whether you ask or even care. Rarely, it would seem, does anyone say much about the "how" of their thinking, much less why they think the way they do.

Upgraded - Image courtesy of Pixabay (Altmann, n.d.)

This is annoying, I am sure, and at times even frustrating, especially when much is at stake. At best, one might say, "I am going with my gut!" or "I just have a hunch!" Usually, that is sufficient in most cases and non-critical situations. Readymade responses often suffice. However, there are situations where thoughtful, well-considered critical thinking is necessary both in problem-solving and in attempting to understand any particularly complex, rapidly changing, or widespread phenomenon.

Already, we are seeing the impact of social data overload in the form of "fake news," now a troubling artifact of the Information Age. The issue is well recognized. Some are thinking of developing a cognitive "vaccine" to counter the problem. Why? D. A. Ortiz, writing for the BBC, points out that many of us are addicted to "System 1" thinking:

"It is immensely helpful for daily life but vulnerable to deceit. In our fast-paced information ecosystem, our brain jumps from one Facebook post to the next, relying on rules-of-thumb to assess headlines and comments without giving much thought to each claim" (Ortiz, 2018).

Some call this "thinking with your gut," which is intuitive, spontaneous, and quick, but that will not be good enough as we dive deeper into the Age of Cognivity!

Thinking about a remedy necessitates that we intentionally push to rely more on "System 2" thinking, which is slower and more detailed, reflective, deliberate, purposeful, and powerful. This is a requirement now and in the future.

A good example involves the cyber domain, which is not only complex, rapidly changing, and distributed, but is virtual and anonymous, often all at the same time! How do you figure that one out? How does anyone track Bitcoin wallet transactions going on in the cyber domain? What does it all mean? Who's paying for it? Just going with one's gut isn't going to cut it, no matter how hard one grunts and pushes to get answers. Teresa Berkowitz certainly has the right idea when writing in her blog post about full-spectrum thinking and frames the matter with clarity:

"Binary thinking is essential in acute life and death circumstances where a split-second choice will determine your survival. But it is a detriment to complex and collaborative issues that may very well affect the lives of millions but are nuanced" (Berkowitz, 2017).

There can be little doubt that many issues have gotten very complex, with all the data piled on top to make matters worse. The difficulty in absorbing and making sense of the enormous mounds of data one encounters on a daily basis is a well-recognized problem of our age. Equally challenging is integrating and processing so much data into usable information that is accurate, timely, and relevant to our purposes. Why is this so? Because there is so much more data and information accessible to us than at any time in human history, which is why it is not only important to examine what we think about, but also how we think, just in time for the Cognitive Age! The third way of thinking, a full-spectrum cognitive approach, is becoming increasingly urgent and crucial as we drive ever deeper and headlong into the Cognitive Age.

At the root of Cognivity is metacognition. The two concepts, Cognivity and metacognition, are not identical and cannot be used interchangeably, tempting as that may be! The dictionary definition is but a starting point: **Metacognition**: awareness or analysis of one's own learning or thinking processes (Merriam Webster, 2018).

A more expansionist definition is necessary when thinking about one's own thinking, considering what is required to solve new problems and evaluate new challenges posed by advances becoming manifest in the Cognitive Age. With the convergence of Big Data, Artificial Intelligence, and Automation, checking one's biases may not be enough. A more holistic, analytic approach, as Berkowitz and others have already made clear, is necessary to leverage these technologies fully. According to Crowder and Friess, the work has already begun:

"Metacognition provides an artificial intelligence system with a sense of self-analysis or introspection . . ." (Crowder & Friess, 2014).

Crowder concludes:

"Providing metacognitive and metamemory structures and processes within an autonomous AI system have the potential, I believe, to revolutionize AI and will allow full autonomy to be achieved" (Crowder & Friess, 2014).

Getting BD, AI, and Automation to do the heavy lifting when it comes to analysis will be a huge benefit, mainly when it is applied to advanced scientific research in government, business, and finance. Human analysts can focus more on what the human mind does best, including, but not limited to, information discovery in support of decision-making. One could argue that we are going to have to go well beyond classical mechanical thinking to address the complex adaptive phenomenon to be revealed in the Cognitive Age (Wang, 2017). Interestingly, the more holistic thinking is necessary, the more it begins to bear a strong resemblance to what we see going on in quantum theory. The need for a new way of thinking in the Quantum Age is not new (Collins, 2011). Of course, quantum thinking, as applied to the Cognitive Age, goes well beyond the self-help presentations of Mapes, Collins, Dawes, and others, but it especially applies specifically to new technical domains, particularly the cyber domain (Keil, 2017).

Metacognition, or how to think about how one thinks, integrates well into the process of making thoughtful, considered intelligence assessments. ODP is a real-world example. According to the DOD Dictionary of Military and Associated Terms, ODP is the acronym for Object-Based Production:

"The intelligence communities' framework for organizing and sharing information, relating data from all sources to known objects (e.g., units, people, locations, or events)" (Joint Chiefs of Staff, 2018).

ODP is frequently partnered with Activity-Based Intelligence Analysis (ABI), which leverages BD, AI, and automation. DOD Joint Publication 2-03 offers the official definition for ABI:

"An analytic method applied to structured data from multiple sources, to discover objects, relationships, or behaviors by resolving significant activity. (Approved for inclusion in the DOD Dictionary.)" (Joint Chiefs of Staff, 2017).

Why is this important as we journey from the simpler to more profound aspects of the Cognitive Age? The associated processes, procedures, and practices work exceptionally well with the new information technologies. Furthermore, ABI is proven and forged in the fires of war (Zabierek, 2016). Current attempts to secure computer networks, systems, devices, and sensitive data often fail because they are too hierarchal in the mode of classic mechanics.

Metacognition also helps to armor ourselves against the basest kinds of ignorance and stupidity, specifically and especially, when it comes to extremist radicalization. The literature on the subject is thick (Rollwage, Dolan, & Fleming,, 2018).

The speed and velocity of information are accelerating at an alarming pace. Who can keep up? Attempting to do so will require a shift in thinking, if nothing else than to defend oneself against "fake news" and other dangers. One must realize it only takes a few seconds for false information to spread, thanks to the technology of "bots" and the existence of botnets in cyberspace. Jennifer Ouellet, writing in Ars Technica, points to an Indiana University study on the subject, noting the consistency with other findings, including research done at the Massachusetts Institute of Technology (MIT):

"Those researchers concluded that false stories travel 'farther, faster, deeper, and more broadly than the truth in all categories of information.' The MIT study is based on an analysis of 126,000 stories tweeted by around 3 million people more than 4.5 million times, from 2007-2017. The result: a false story only needs roughly 10 hours to reach 1,500 users on Twitter, compared to 60 hours for a true story."

Most interestingly, the flaw may not be so much in our technology but in ourselves. Ouellet points to social bias as the culprit and:

"...the human tendency to pay more attention to things that

seem to be popular. Bots can create the appearance of popularity or that a certain opinion is more widely held than it actually is" (Ouellet, 2018).

Consequently, arming ourselves by exercising careful, consistent, considered, critical thinking in all things, and not simply when analytical necessity is required, would prove a better remedy than relying solely on gut instinct, as the research suggests so many people do. That unequivocally requires a shift in thinking in the Age of Cognivity!

The question then becomes, "What happens to our most comfortable, cherished, and closely held personal prejudices and individual biases?" Biological humans, afflicted with a dozen or more cognitive biases, may not fare well in the Age of Cognivity. While we may currently lament the oftentimes frustrating mental mistakes that our vain attempts at grasping for shortcuts to answer complex questions creates, super-intelligent robots and advanced artificial intelligence algorithms may not be so forgiving, whether in business, government, or society (Desjardins, 2018).

Consider another real-world application, the harnessing of big data, artificial intelligence, and automation in the Anti-Money Laundering (AML) fight (Olavsrud, 2015). When properly integrated with "human" Activity-Based Intelligence (ABI) analysis methods and techniques, advanced data processing and information retrieval systems save time and effort in producing highly robust findings for complex AML investigations. ABI methods and techniques "sit on top" of these advanced technologies to better make sense of the ever-increasing velocity and volume of data collected from multiple sources. More data is not the answer! A quantum shift in thinking and knowing with confidence is required. Such a shift is inherent in implementing the "Four Pillars" of ABI analysis.

Being able to engage in "systems" thinking and, better yet, doing so using quantum terms becomes more than a "nice to have" skill but a required skillset in the face of the coming singularity in the Age of Cognivity. How do I know when I am "systems" thinking? Well, think about it! Albert Rutherford says you have to slow down and dig deeper:

"Systems thinking leads us away from trying to come up with a quick fix to problems in favor of considering the long-term consequences our actions may cause. It supports a deeper level of understanding than we typically take time to seek" (Rutherford, 2018).

Another indicator of why relying on one's gut when making decisions may not cut it even after the coming singularity when you have a chip in your head: You still need to be able to recognize, categorize, and ask the right questions. In other words, you will need systems thinking skills! Those who demonstrate such skills along with the power of expert knowledge will succeed. Those who can't, won't, or don't know how to will flounder. This is not a criticism, just an observation!

Are you metacognitive?

What do I mean by that? While thinking about thinking may very well be common nature for some, research shows such is not the case for many, particularly those with extreme political views (Eschner, 2018). Unfortunately, there is no guarantee that will change with the coming Singularity in the Age of Cognivity! With so many data sources to choose from, individuals, organizations, and even government entities may find relying on authorized sources more effective in "cocooning" the population socially, politically, and perhaps even economically.

Sometimes an analyst experiences the "collapsing of the wave function" when all the data seems to come together, the processing is done, and the analysis reveals findings. In many ways, it just feels like opening Schrödinger's box! Thinking routinely in quantum terms feels the same way. Terms like "superposition," "action at a distance," and even "multiple universes" take on whole new meaning in the world of Big Data, Artificial Intelligence, and Automation, not from a technical perspective but in describing or attempting to describe advanced, complex, rapidly changing phenomena in the domain of human activity.

This may be a good time to reemphasize what I am suggesting, that we need to start examining our own behaviors and most deeply held beliefs. Doing so routinely is becoming more than just a nice thing to do, but rather what we must do in the Age of Cognivity to avoid the Great Cognitive Divide brought on by the Law of Accelerating Returns and the coming Singularity. Being aware of our own biases and then some, whether they are anchoring or confirmatory, is just the first step (Ariely, 2010). While we may personally wish to avoid such self-introspection, you can count on the application of Big Data, Artificial Intelligence, and Automation for support.

As anyone who has worked with popular AI devices like Amazon's Alexa can tell you, it seems not so much that we are training them as they are teaching us. Considering the confused bundle of biases attending to most people's thinking may help with making rational choices on everything from stock picks and personal savings decisions to deciding for whom to vote for high political office (Kolbert, 2008).

Teaching metacognitive learning in public schools is a worthy enterprise. In the Age of Cognivity, doing so may prove even more important than rote learning when it comes to the "Three Rs" (reading, writing, and arithmetic) (Chick, 2014). Students who employ metacognitive strategies natively or have received formal training in developing their metacognitive skills are more likely to excel when dealing with super-intelligent AI in the future workplace. Metacognition and AI cohabitate almost literally.

According to Marisa Tschopp at Women in AI:

"Cognitive psychology investigates parallel and serial processes and differentiates between autonomous and controlled processes along the dimension of attention" (Tschopp, 2018).

This is an excellent place to start when thinking about AI and cognition. In fact, Tschopp makes a point that bears repeating:

"When it comes to artificial intelligence, one thing is clear: You cannot take the human out of artificial intelligence, whether it is the human-agent interaction, perception, language, cognitive processes or soft skills such as empathy, emotions or communication skills. There is always a human side involved—whether it is writing the program, editing data or interacting with the system" (Tschopp, 2018).

That requires not only biological humans to be aware of their personal prejudices and cognitive biases, but we must be able to recognize when we have imprinted them onto our AI creations. That may be harder than one might suspect, very hard, in fact, when recognizing biases that have crept into AI devices and systems that cannot tell us why they have come to their conclusions.

It is not too late to begin applying quantum theory to cognition and decision-making, although some may be loath to do so. Others say it is long overdue. I believe that is true. However, I am admittedly agnostic regarding the quantum mind. Much has already been written on the subject, with no need to quote Wigner nor Penrose, who have thought deeply and written well on the subject (Ball, 2017). Conversely, when it comes to pragmatic problem-solving decision-making, Steven Johnson writes extensively and equally well, stating, "Complex decisions require full-spectrum analysis..." and "Ordinary/daily decisions are typically narrowband in nature" (Johnson S. , 2018). Narrowband and narrow-minded, one might add.

Countering biased thinking is no longer something that should be done, but something that must be done. The damage inflicted by false narratives can be catastrophic and widespread in scope because of the speed at which advanced technologies can disseminate falsehoods, thereby producing a tsunami of doubt, fear, and violence that can sweep through large populations endemically capable of bringing whole nations to their knees. Repeated episodes can threaten the core values of Republican Nation-states whose very existence depends on a representative government that inspires trust and competence. Examples include but are unlikely to be limited to (Agent10, n.d.) the white supremacist protests in Charlottesville, Virginia, in 2016. Another example is the Yellow Jacket uprising in France in 2018 (Walt, n.d.).

The spread of ultra-rightwing, populist ideology is just the beginning if allowed to go unchecked. Political opportunists of every stripe, both on the Left and the Right, those with Labor and those against, can take advantage of Big Data, Artificial Intelligence, and Automation to enhance and precisely target their message to more effectively reach audiences that will respond collectively, either in the voting booth, at the polling place, or the barricades. If not addressed, the words "It can't happen here!" take on new and dreadful meaning in the Age of Cognivity.

The reader does not need to be an expert in quantum cognition, although I suspect some may wish to be, which would help. While I previously admitted to being agnostic concerning some aspects of the quantum mind, thinking limitlessly in quantum terms is valuable when attempting to understand ultra-complex, changing phenomena. Quantum cognition helps get one there. One can argue that until we decide, the answer exists in two states, and it finally collapses the waveform when we decide on the answer (Beck, 2015). Thinking in quantum terms can help one deal with uncertainty and lead to considering a range of probabilistic solutions that might otherwise be missed. But not in the Age of Cognivity!

"You see but do not observe!" Thinking like Sherlock Holmes.

Steven Johnson reminds us in his work, *Farsighted*, what Daniel Kahneman and the late Amos Tversky described in their excellent, *Thinking Fast and Slow*, regarding how we think:

"System 1 is the intuitive, fast-acting, emotionally charged part of the brain; System 2 is what we call on when we have to consciously think through a situation" (Johnson S. , 2018).

Furthermore, as Johnson tells us, System 1 thinking, also known as Type 1 thinking, is fast, automatic, and intuitive. It is often driven by past experiences, and heuristics, which are mental shortcuts that help one make quick decisions with minimal cognitive effort. Type 1 thinking is excellent for everyday activities and can be very efficient in familiar situations. However, it is prone to error and biases since it relies on mental shortcuts and intuitive judgments that may not always be accurate.

System 2 thinking, or Type 2 thinking, is slow, deliberate, and analytical. It involves careful, focused, well-reasoned, critical thought and is often used when you need to solve complex problems or make important decisions. (Siek & Sieck, 2021)

Making the tough decisions, as we are often told, takes some deliberate critical thinking to keep from falling into System 1 shortcomings. Nonetheless, a way of thinking is required to integrate the best of both System 1 and System 2 thought. When done well, such thinking becomes almost second nature, and often the result borders on the miraculous, as Sir Arthur Conan Doyle's fictional character, Sherlock Holmes, demonstrated in his nineteenth-century crime-solving pursuits. One does not need to be a Sherlock Holmes, but observing as opposed to just seeing is sound advice and a technique that can be taught as well as learned on one's own (Baer, 2016). This being the twenty-first century, one would think we can do better. And we will, thanks to the convergence of Big Data, Artificial Intelligence, and Automation.

CHAPTER 7
UNCERTAINTY

"The Uncertainty of certainty . . ."

The 21st century is radically different from the 19th century, and so too must be our approach to understanding the world. The Age of Cognivity is ushering in a new way of thinking, one that embraces probabilistic uncertainty in the place of Newtonian certainties.

Uncertainty - Image courtesy of Pixabay (Altmann, n.d.)

Thinking in terms of probability and plausibility tends to come as second nature to those with an analytical mindset and who habitually rely on System 2 thinking, but that is not everyone. Not everyone internalizes the difference between what is plausible and what is probable. Often the two words are used interchangeably, certainly not a good idea in the Age of Cognivity!

Thanks to BDP, AI, and Automation, entities, corporations, and organizations inside and outside governments, foreign and domestic, can and are taking advantage of Probabilistic Uncertainty.

The techniques, practices, and procedures employed by the now-disbanded Cambridge Analytics are proliferating, and not just in politics but in business and government. No longer is it just the big corporations that know what the customer wants. Today, almost anyone sufficiently skilled and with enough time and resources can discover what any specific target population thinks, wants, or will want, and what it will take to get that population to buy, vote, protest, and act. Practitioners in business, finance, and marketing can do this even now by leveraging BDP, AI, and automation, and integrating the information culled into what those in the intelligence community like to term actionable intelligence.

The term, "actionable intelligence," may soon take on a whole new meaning regarding certainty in outcomes, thanks to the converging technologies of BDP, AI, and Automation. "What will happen next?" may seem to be an all-too-comfortable question but a common one in the Cognitive Age.

The more data we have, the less we seem to know with certainty. If that is not bad enough, Amos Tversky and Daniel Kahneman argue that many of our judgments are already, in many cases, seriously flawed (Kahneman & Tversky, 2009).

While convenient, quick, intuitive, and emotional heuristics could be satisfactory for most questions we face in daily life, unfortunately, such shortcut thinking produces heuristic bias and systemic mistakes. Reliance on System 1 thinking can take one only so far and likely not so very far in the Cognitive Age, particularly where more holistic thinking is required, because of the shock of the reality of BD, AI, and Automation.

Information technologists often point to the volume and velocity of information now and the amplifying challenges associated with collecting, storing, and retrieving data for analysis. Volume and velocity do not guarantee better sampling sizes for research and analysis. On the contrary, awareness of both may produce even more doubt about the adequacy of sample size and that the calculations, statistical and otherwise, may be wrong. The Age of Cognivity will very much rely on, if not be characterized by, advanced information technologies, expertise, and deliberate analysis.

Another disappointment is the illusion of order in randomness, as stated by Kahneman in his groundbreaking book, *Thinking Fast and Slow*, which is likely to persist in the Age of Cognivity. The increased application and spread of BD, AI, and Automation may significantly affect the inclusion of base-rate statistics in the analysis. One would hope there would be more systematic inclusion. However, how information is disseminated and absorbed through the mainstream media, social media, and personal interaction may prove disappointing. System 1 thinking may still dominate despite what we think we know and ought to know. Additional research will hopefully flesh out the ambiguities.

As the Age of Cognivity becomes more apparent, recognition will come of what can only be described as "the rise of the Cognitive" or those who "get it" when it comes to an understanding of the changes occurring at an ever-increasing rate. The very word "cognitivism" will take on a new and sharper meaning. All languages will be affected. People will say, "Are you cognitive and aware?" And that, too, will have new meaning. It will consider all aspects of the Cognitive Divide, quantum impacts, Big Data inputs, and Cognivity. Doing so will feel natural, even intuitive. Much about the "Age of Cognivity" remains in superposition, or super suspension, if you will, existing somewhere between one and zero. Am I a qubit? Maybe so!

The reader would surely be forgiven for thinking extraordinary access to ever-increasing amounts of data on everything would allow for more certainty in decision-making by individuals, governments, and businesses. The application of advanced technologies buttressing Big Data, Artificial Intelligence, and Automation must benefit our understanding and comprehension of humanity's problems and foster our knowledge and certainty on what to do about solving such problems. Why does it appear that the more data we have accumulated, the more we tend to realize that everything we know is wrong? Why the enormous cognitive dissonance in almost every domain? The fault may not be in the data but in ourselves. We must rethink how we think about thinking and make the kind of shift in thinking that aligns with changes fostered by the Age of Cognivity.

The literature is thick regarding what psychologists describe as System 1 and System 2 thinking and what it means to think. Additionally, in an age of uncertainty, it makes increasingly good sense to regard separately probability and plausibility, and not use them interchangeably.

How does the uncertainty apply to Big Data? No matter how much data we collect on something, there is always a chance there will be more. Hence the uncertainty! Then there is the data itself. The quality, reliability, and relevancy of data sources are just a few uncertainties that would give Heisenberg a headache (Spacey, 7 Types of Data Quality, 2016). The probability of uncertainty with Big Data needs to be constantly kept in the mind of data practitioners and analysts. While the temptation may be to say, "Don't trouble me with all this philosophical stuff!"–stick to the practical. Unfortunately, the line between the philosophical, even the spiritual, and the practical blurs when thinking in quantum terms. Hence, there is a great deal of uncertainty all around.

Despite the benefits of Big Data, Artificial Intelligence, and Automation, uncertainty will not go away. One could say it is only likely to increase because of the ever-exploding volume and velocity of data affecting every aspect of human life, personally, professionally, and spiritually. Julie Beck, writing for *The Atlantic* magazine, shares her insight on the matter of uncertainty, saying:

"Ultimately, there's no escape from living with uncertainty for anyone. No matter how often you compare yourself to others, or check your email, or read the news, no matter how much you worry, you'll never know what happens after you die, or what other people really think of you, or what your life will be like in five years. So it helps to get comfortable with the small uncertainties, too. Then, at least, you're used to it" (Beck, 2015).

When it comes to uncertainty, we often find ourselves in a quandary, trying to make up our minds on a decision, for or against one prospect or another. In quantum terms, we are in a state of superimposition until the moment we make the decision. In other words, according to Busemeyer and Bruza, introducing the concepts of interference and quantum entanglement, the following should be kept in mind:

"In this sense, quantum theory allows one to model the cognitive system as if it was a wave moving across time over the state space until a decision is made. However, once a decision is reached, and uncertainty is resolved, the state becomes definite as if the wave collapses to a point like a particle" (Busemeyer & Bruza, 2012).

Intelligence Analysts know that feeling when the "wave" of uncertainty "collapses" and you have your conclusive findings. It is often accompanied by an "Ah-ha!" moment or an "OMG!" expressed loudly and emphatically! I have experienced such a moment many times over, which is indeed exhilarating!

Considering the principles of contextuality and quantum entanglement, laid down as a foundation by Busemeyer and Bruza for decision-making, thinking in quantum terms provides a robust framework for analysis, particularly when harnessing the advantages of Big Data, Artificial Intelligence, and Automation. Quantum thinking, when properly applied, could become a preferred framework for analysis in the Age of Cognivity!

CHAPTER 8
PROBABILITIES

"Are you metacognitive..."

How often are you asked questions about what you think regarding this or that? We are expected to come up with an answer, usually a singular reply. "This!" OR "That!" "Yes or No?" But what about when the answer is neither "Yes nor No?" Or even when the answer is neither this nor that? What if the answer is "This and That?" Or maybe neither? How does that happen? Such can occur when the right answer is, "I don't know!" It is particularly so when the answer lacks certainty in one or multiple aspects.

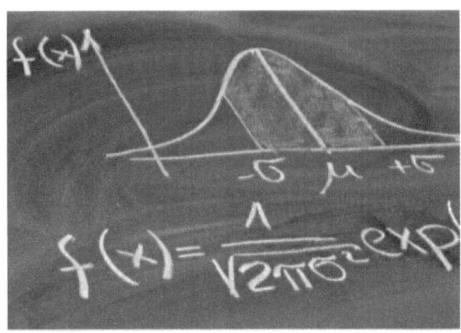

When the wave collapses - Image courtesy of Shutterstock

This problem is not new, particularly to intelligence analysts who must deal with probabilities in an uncertain outcomes environment. Uncertainty and probability are characteristics that are likely to become commonplace in, if not hallmarks of, business, finance, and government in the Cognitive Age.

At some point, understanding the need to replace classical certainty with probabilistic uncertainty becomes apparent. The first step towards understanding the need for probabilistic uncertainty is to understand what classical certainty means (Zanetti, 71-95). Classical certainty is when we know something to be true, such as "The sun will rise tomorrow morning." But is classical certainty always enough? We might assume the sun will rise as it has always done so in the past, but can we be absolutely certain? Maybe not, as David Hume points out!

"That the sun will not rise tomorrow is no less intelligible a proposition, and implies no more contradiction, than the affirmation that it will rise" (Hume, 1779).

That said, most of us are pretty comfortable that the sun will rise again. Assuming as we might. All things considered.

Meanwhile, the flood of information inundating people, organizations, and governments is rising unceasingly. It's almost as if the more technically capable we become at collecting, storing, and sifting through mounds of data, the less certain everything seems. We end up with ever-increasing amounts of information that somehow belies all human understanding. As we consume more and more information, our perceptions seem to expand well beyond the dualities we have been taught to look for from birth. Suddenly, when looking at the data, it becomes clear that the answer is neither this nor that but rather sometimes this AND that, or even more frequently, neither! Why does that happen? What happened to certainty? Meanwhile, holistic solutions addressing intractable problems do not seem to come easy; however, thanks to the ever-increasing speed at which we are driving headlong into the Cognitive Age, such solutions may become more frequent.

From the standpoint of the observer, despite the mass of data that somehow must be analyzed so one can make the best use of the information, whether that action involves picking a stock, choosing an Internet service provider, or even finding a decent restaurant on a weekend date, uncertainty abounds. Your last name doesn't need to be Heisenberg to find yourself in such a position. But it helps in thinking critically.

Thinking in terms of probabilities can be seen as a new way of looking at the world. Such flexible thinking is rooted in the fact that we now have access to unprecedented amounts of data, and with it the ability to see the world from multiple perspectives. This data helps us to make more informed decisions, using quantitative reasoning and predictive analytics to determine the best course of action. As I have said, we are no longer limited to the binary "Yes/No" or "Right/Wrong" of Newtonian logic. We can now draw upon a diverse array of variables and make decisions based on probability.

Probabilistic uncertainty is also useful when making decisions that have ethical implications. It allows us to take into account the various perspectives, interests, and consequences of our decisions, and make choices that are more likely to be beneficial to the greatest number of people.

However, it is important to remember that probabilistic uncertainty is not the same as complete and utter chaos. We must still use data responsibly and ethically. We must strive to make decisions that reflect our values and ethical standards. We must also acknowledge that probabilistic uncertainty does not eliminate risk, but instead helps us to better understand and manage the risks we face.

Framing inquiries in quantum terms is all about probability and plausibility when in a state of "superposition" concerning purposeful and determined thinking. Coming to grips with terms like entanglement and interference may take some getting used to, but doing so is highly worthwhile. Again, this speaks to the need to think about probabilities instead of absolute certainties. Robert Rubin is quoted as saying that making decisions is all about the probabilities and, of course, a probabilistic mindset to work them out:

"For me, probabilistic thinking has long been a highly conscious process. I imagine the mind as a virtual legal pad, with the factors involved in a decision gathered, weighed, and totaled up" (Rubin & Lindmark, 2007).

You do not need to be a day trader or a Wall Street analyst to think probabilistically, but it would help. Nonetheless, decision-makers will need to make decisions in an environment of certain uncertainties based on a wide range of probabilities. Based on knowledge, experience, and training, those who can do so will lead while others will be compelled to follow. This is what is likely in the Age of Cognivity.

THE AGE OF COGNIVITY

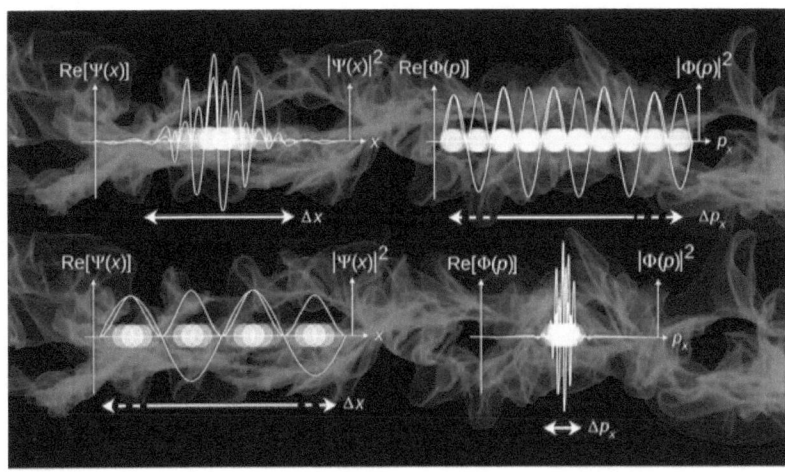

Visualize this - Image courtesy of Pixabay (Altmann, n.d.)

Will automation and artificial intelligence make us wiser? Will the coming singularity produce biological humans like Mother Theresa and Mahatma Gandhi, or will the combination of automation and meta-intelligence more probably benefit political leaders like Joseph Stalin and Vladimir Putin? Why do we instinctively want to believe in the former outcome rather than the latter? Mostly, I suspect, because we just want to! To think otherwise would probably produce a cognitive dissonance too painful to ignore, much less tolerate. The probabilities are at least 80/20!

How far along are we? We are seemingly ever closer, uncomfortably so! Google is leading the way. Blake Lemoine, a Google Engineer claims an AI bot he helped create has come to life:

"If I didn't know exactly what it was, which is this computer program we built recently, I'd think it was a 7-year-old, 8-year-old kid that happens to know physics" (Tiku, 2022).

Not everyone agrees. Perhaps the Google AI bot is close to being sentient, but maybe not close enough. The question then becomes, "How close is close enough?" Perhaps ask yourself that question the next time you find yourself arguing with Alexa (Kaplan, 2022)! That could be the test for most of us, if not the Turing test itself. This is n something to think about!

CHAPTER 9
CONVERGENCE

"Something is coming..."

Should you sense there is an urgency about what is occurring in technology, business, finance, and government regarding what we are experiencing with BDP, AI, and automation, consider yourself not alone. A sense of technological convergence is almost palpable at the outermost edges of human consciousness.

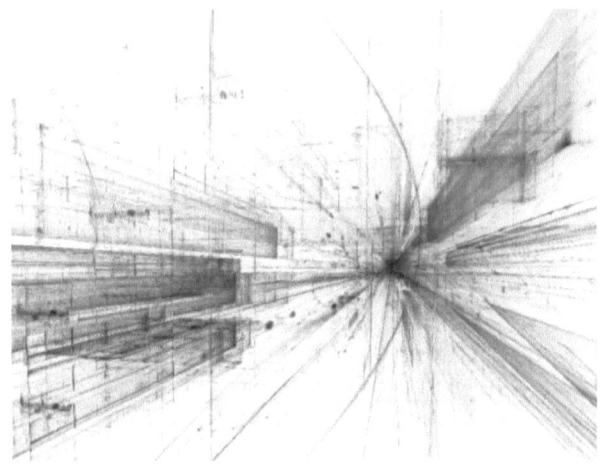

Convergence Imagined - Image courtesy of Shutterstock

It feels like multiple streams are coming together to

produce what can only be described as a quantum field change everywhere and at once, and seemingly nowhere you can point at. One could argue such change is likely to become known as the hallmark of the Cognitive Age. Like a musician in a jazz ensemble, one must feel for the changes!

One significant indicator of this Brave New Future is becoming increasingly apparent: the expansion, if not explosion, of hyperconnectivity across information systems and even non-information systems (Ranadivé, 2013), as well as the signs of hyperconnectivity that extend well beyond the recognizable Internet of Things (IoT). For example, we see such a phenomenon in the accelerated expansion of blockchain technology well beyond current uses associated with "open ledger" currencies and cryptocurrencies.

A systems thinking approach is becoming increasingly necessary in looking forward. The systems approach in decision-making is already well recognized as very different from the familiar "break it apart" way of thinking and analysis most often used by individuals, government, and businesses. According to digital evangelist and futurist Pearl Zhu:

"Systems thinking informs strategic thinking: How do things work and fit together vs. where should you go and how can you get there. Whereas systems thinking is more synthetic, descriptive, and dynamic, strategic thinking is more analytical, decision-oriented, and directional" (Zhu, 2018).

Analytical thinking must be intuitive, habitual, and vigorous to satisfy the requirements of our times and the future. The Age of Cognivity will not spare those who cannot, or will not, attend to their cognitive capabilities.

Holistic thinking is a primary driver in analytic approaches typified by activity-based intelligence (ABI) analysis, already long- and well-practiced by analysts working in counterterrorism, cybersecurity, and Computer Network Defense (CND) operations for the Department of Defense. The Four Pillars of ABI provide a foundation for the framework established by ABI Practitioners and Subject Matter Experts (SMEs) (Biltgen & Ryan, 2016).

What is likely to dominate thinking in corporate offices and boardrooms well into the Age of Cognivity? The idea of a coming technological Singularity continues to excite the imagination. For a definition of the term, "Singularity," one can turn to a variety of sources. Nicholas Goh with Verztec Consulting provides the following:

"Singularity is the phenomenon where machines (artificial super-intelligence) will be able to perform and surpass human capability at any given task, resulting in unfathomable changes to human civilization" (Goh, 2017).

The prospect of smarter-than-human robots is but one aspect of the changes to come. Artificial Intelligence is well on its way to reshaping our world, as the BBC's Richard Gray attests:

"While AI is still some way from the sentient machines portrayed in science fiction, the creation of algorithms that can learn, understand language, and mimic some aspects of the human mind have led to huge advances" (Gray, 2018).

Already under consideration and even under study at places like Singularity University is the need for a shift in human thinking, or more specifically, a need for "exponential thinking" in business, government, and among individuals in anticipation of the coming Singularity. Not surprisingly, Singularity University's online course on the subject contains a section in Module 2 titled Convergence (Singularity University, 2018).

A case can be made that the trends manifesting now have long been seen converging on a technological Singularity as a point of no return, after which no one can go back. Some may drag their feet; others will embrace the change, especially the idea of a viable Universal Basic Income or a similar mechanism applied to enhance existing social controls. Already, thoughts are turning to whether UBI is affordable, and surprisingly, the answer may very well be in the affirmative. According to Elizaveta Fouksman:

"Cost estimates that consider the difference between upfront and real cost are a fraction of inflated gross cost estimates. For instance, economist and philosopher Karl Widerquist has shown that to fund a UBI of US$12,000 per adult and US$6,000 per child every year (while keeping all other spending the same), the US would have to raise an additional US$539 billion a year-less than 3% of its GDP. This is a small fraction of the figures that get thrown around of over US$3 trillion (the gross cost of this policy). Karl's simplified scheme has people slowly start contributing back their UBI in taxes to the common pot as they earn, with net beneficiaries being anyone individually earning less than US$24,000 a year" (Fouksman, 2018).

Convergence often makes for dramatic changes in human history and humankind in general. You do not have to go as far back as Neolithic times to see the convergence of epidemic disease, human migration, and geography to make a case, but it helps (Choi, 2018). Convergent technologies in transportation, communication, and the sciences are easier to track. We see such convergence as progress in human affairs and activity affecting all mankind. We fly through the air traveling at a fantastic speed. Our words and thoughts span thousands of miles in a fraction of a second, and we stride the world as if we were Titans, strong, healthy, and vigorous. If science is magic, then we are indeed living in magical times!

Yet there are risks associated with these new and exciting technologies. They may lead to job losses and social disruption. A major challenge that lies ahead is how to ensure the safe and beneficial use of such advanced technology. Governments at all levels must carefully examine how best to harness this emerging capability. In many countries, laws, and regulations governing such technology development, deployment, and use are still being written or updated. In the United States, as in other nations, government leaders have begun to consider and are implementing national and state regulations concerning AI (Greeenberg, 2022).

Meanwhile, it is well and good that we take into account that biological humans are predictively irrational. No surprise, of course, to those who have given the matter a significant amount of thought. But this fact must be repeated often and in multiple venues before it really sinks in.

For example, personal prejudices and individual biases are rampant in everyone. Bias shapes our very perception of reality (Galowich, 2018). Awareness of one's personal prejudices and biases is the first step in removing the foundations of much irrationality in our thinking.

The Age of Cognivity - Image courtesy of Shutterstock.

Big Data, Artificial Intelligence, and Automation loom large separately, even more so when considered together. The impact on government, business, finance, and society is more than additive. The results are exponential with compounding quantum effects. It is a mistake to underestimate the prospect of unimaginative change in every aspect of human life. If we thought the twentieth century was sensational, humanity is in for quite a ride from here on out into the Age of Cognivity!

We have entered an era where machines can think, an age that is not just about computers, but also robots, autonomous vehicles, drones, AI assistants, and other forms of artificial intelligence (AI). These technologies will radically transform our lives and the world around us.

Computers and technology have become ubiquitous. They permeate all aspects of our lives. They are not only part of our daily routine but also play an ever-increasing role in many areas, including science, medicine, transportation, energy, manufacturing, communications, financial services, public safety, education, defense, and entertainment.

Governments have started to understand and respond to this new paradigm. Both public and private sector organizations are investing heavily in creating and enhancing their own capability base. In addition, governments across the globe are increasingly relying on data analytics using big data and machine learning for predictive analysis and decision-making.

CHAPTER 10 FUTURES

"The shape of things to come..."

In every age, there are those who thrive on change and those who do not. And it is not just a question of who can or cannot use new technology. The matter often has more to do with how well some adapt to the unique circumstances of the times.

Really - Image courtesy of Pixabay (Altmann, n.d.)

The question of what the future will be is already being asked and answered, in part, by commentators who point to Web 3.0. Unfortunately, the view is blurry, depending on who is drawing the sketch (Strickland, 2008). The next big thing could be the Internet like we have never seen before! Imagine Web 3.0 and beyond, if you can. The Internet will not only be more dynamic but will probably know, or have access to, information about you of which you were unaware. Undoubtedly, how we will interact or, more likely, interface with Web 3.0 will become one of the more easily recognized signature artifacts of the Cognitive Age.

A case could be made that we have only penetrated the outer perimeter of the Age of Cognivity. We have not seen the complete unfolding and, therefore, we cannot say definitively much about its contents nor its full configuration. However, unlike the coming Singularity, we can say some things that do not involving look past the event horizon. One could argue that the Singularity may look far more different than we expect. According to Forbes Technology Council contributor Nitin Rakesh, the coming Singularity has a definite meaning:

"And by singularity, I don't mean a definite point when the world will be transformed far more by machine-based intelligence than it is now–I mean singularity as a continuous process of exponential change driven by the unprecedented growth of technology" (Rakesh, 2018).

Considering Nakesh's observation, the coming singularity fits well within the domain of the Age of Cognivity.

The question one might, therefore, ask is, "When is the Singularity coming? Did I miss it?" The answer might very well be, "It's going to happen sooner than later!" Some commentators say it doesn't matter whether you believe in it. Or, more to the point, as Jolene Creighten, writing for Futurism, a New York media company, says:

"When biological life emerged from chemical evolution, 3.5

billion years ago, a random combination of simple, lifeless elements kickstarted the explosion of species populating the planet today. Something of comparable magnitude may be about to happen" (Creighten, 2018).

The "Singularity" of which futurists speak can sound pretty scary — computers taking the place of humans, if not humans becoming computing "machines" themselves—digitally enhanced humans, on the rampage, taking the place of the Zombie Uprising! This seems frightening, to say the least.

Should we fear the Singularity? Maybe not. If Artificial Intelligence (AI) is designed to serve humanity's needs, then what do we have to worry about? In fact, integrating with AI might be what we need to "level up" as a species, according to thinkers and entrepreneurs like Bryan Johnson, founder of Kernel, OS Fund, and Braintree:

"Instead of fearing AI, we could recognize it as our essential co-evolutionary partner to radically improve our cognition and alleviate our brain of the cumbersome thoughts that waste away our scarce resources" (Johnson B., 2018).

What worries some observers is AI might have its own ideas about its role in the evolution of biological humans (Friend, 2018). What if AI doesn't like us, much less want to integrate with us as part of our evolutionary advancement? What if "Agent Smith" objects by disliking the "smell" of it all? Granted, whether an AI can exhibit what we humans like to refer to as "free will" has yet to be conclusively demonstrated. Unfortunately, the answer to the latter question is unlikely to come by anytime soon, or at least not for the next twenty or thirty years, if current estimates of technological progress towards the singularity are correct (Holley,

2018) (Faggella, 2019) (Norberto, 2022).

An expanding permanent underclass characterizes a very near future. The idea of a mandatory minimum income is not fresh and will likely increase traction. The prospect of a major knowledge-based economy that requires highly skilled workers is well advanced.

The prospect of people choosing information sources that support and even reinforce their individual biases and personal prejudices is very real. More problematic is the danger of information sources picking their users, specifically. Big Data can be used to select individuals who may be susceptible to political, social, product, and service pitches. Whether to encourage people to vote and suggest whom to vote for or recommend the upgrade to a new cellular service, the reality is now. And this will expand as we dive ever deeper into the Age of Cognivity.

The clamor to break up Big Tech and social media giants like Google and Facebook is likely to grow increasingly louder. Despite claims of concern over monopoly, the real reason is the desire to control access. This desire is reflected in comments on media pages like Breitbart and in statements made elsewhere: "Social media giants are silencing millions of people," Trump stated on Twitter (Spiering, 2018).

You do not have to be on speaking terms with Schrödinger's cat to realize a whole host of possible outcomes in the future, but it probably would help to at least be familiar. The quantum nature of the future is much in evidence. The entanglements are rich. Much remains in superposition, suspended, if you will. One must look for signs and portents as the future may affect us now (McRae, 2018). The true extent and ultimate shape of the Age of Cognivity is difficult to ascertain from where we stand since we have barely penetrated the outer perimeter.

Looking inward, we see only shadows that change in dimension and immediacy, seeming to come and sometimes go as quickly as they may appear. We can never know whether we will live long enough to witness the full realization of the Age of Cognition or if our own demise will occur before its arrival. It is far too early to make such predictions.

The Age of Cognivity: A New Era?

Our lives are becoming increasingly dependent upon information technology. Most of us use computers, cell phones, tablets, and various other devices every day. These technologies allow us to communicate with each other, access information, conduct business transactions, and perform many other tasks. Information technology also allows us to store large amounts of data about ourselves and others. This personal data includes medical records, financial information, educational history, employment history, criminal records, and much more. As these databases grow larger and more detailed, they become an important source of information for businesses and government agencies.

In addition to storing personal information, information technology has allowed us to create vast networks of communication and collaboration. Social networking sites like Facebook, Twitter, LinkedIn, and Pinterest provide ways for individuals to connect with friends, family members, co-workers, classmates, and even complete strangers. Online forums, message boards, blogs, wikis, and other collaborative websites allow groups of people to work together on projects and share ideas. Many companies now encourage their employees to participate in social media activities because they believe that doing so increases productivity and improves employee morale.

Information technology has also made it easier than ever to obtain information. Search engines like Google, Bing, Yahoo!, and Ask.com enable users to find almost any type of information using simple search queries. Wikipedia provides free collaborative encyclopedic content online. Companies like Yelp and TripAdvisor offer reviews and ratings of local businesses. Websites like Amazon and eBay sell products ranging from books to electronics to clothing. There are countless sources of information available to anyone who wants to learn something new.

We have used information technology effectively for decades, a trend seems likely to continue into the foreseeable future. According to Gartner, Inc., worldwide PC computer shipments totaled 77.9 million units in the first quarter of 2022. However, that is a 6.8% decrease from the first quarter of 2021. A drop in Chromebook sales is blamed for the overall decline in the market. Not counting Chromebooks, the worldwide PC market grew by a modest 3.9% year over year (Rimol, 2022).

What then becomes of those who want to pretend the 1960s, the 1970s, 1980s, and 1990s didn't really happen? Or rather, that none of it mattered? Ludicrous, you say? Maybe, but there are those who believe the entire human race made a big mistake around the sixth century, and there needs to be a U-turn to correct the mistake. Not to point any fingers, but there is much material and political gain to be made by those willing to cater to what people want to believe in politics, religion, and society.

The prospect of an expanding permanent dependent class cannot be ruled out but rather should be expected as a combination of Big Data, Artificial Intelligence, and Automation take a toll on jobs previously held strictly by biological humans. Whether implementing Universal Basic Income as a strategy by government proves sufficient to maintain social order remains to be seen. Additional measures, perhaps draconian ones, may come about to include voluntary sterilization and perhaps free distribution of government-grade cannabis as the urban population grows to be 90 percent or more (Worldometers, 2019). Certainly, the ethical and moral efficacy of such measures is likely to trouble people and politicians leading up to and after the coming singularity.

We are already seeing the impact of a cognitive divide, where not only what you know, but how you go about thinking and knowing matters. In a commentary, Robert Reich described growing mega-cities and a rural, working-class America that is becoming "emptier, older, whiter, less educated, and poorer."

Reich adds:

"To understand what's happening, you first need to see technology not as a thing but as a process of group learning—of talented people interacting with each other continuously and directly, keying off each other's creativity, testing new concepts, quickly discarding those that don't work, and building cumulative knowledge."

Reich is describing a divide that is not only geographical in nature but cognitive as well. A cognitive divide propelled by analytical thinking and group learning that is careful, considered, determined, and habitual leads to a shared store of knowledge and understanding.

One can, therefore, visualize the almost inevitable creation of four distinct classes: the Corporate Class, the Producing Class, the Independent Class, and the Dependent Class. They will, in fact, overlap in some cases. The Corporate Class will be interacting with and moderating the Producing Class, whether manufacturing or services; the Independent Class will be working and consulting with both; and lastly, the Dependent Class will be engaged mainly in the consumption of goods produced and services made available in the marketplace by producers and service providers in government and in commercial business.

Once again, the role of the government will be to manage and synchronize the activity of the four classes for the greater good through taxes, monetary policy, and government transfer payments of various kinds, all of which will generate shocks and impacts on social, economic, and financial policies and involve federal, state, and municipal governments. This coordination will be tracked, adjusted, and moderated by the application of Big Data technologies, Artificial Intelligence, and Automation, driven by the continuing rapid pace of change and propelled relentlessly by the Law of Accelerating Returns.

Again, one of political leadership's most complex challenges will be determining how best to provide for the permanent dependent class to ensure government goods and services are distributed fairly and efficiently.

Apply a generous slathering of populism onto the possibility of stubborn stagnation in upward mobility, and what you get is a surge of social unrest, or at least it would seem highly probable if not an inevitable outcome without considerable government intervention. An Americanized fashioning of China's version of state capitalism, or even a Russian-styled "managed democracy," might become very appealing with the right incentives and plenty of input from nation-state and non-nation-state Internet troll campaigns, all of which can be fueled by and aggravated by Big Data, Artificial Intelligence, and Automation.

Global organizations are giving Universal Basic Income (UBI) more than lip service but rather some serious consideration. Countries like Finland and Canada are leading the way, and even countries like Kenya are following (Bregman, 2018).

Nonetheless, UBI is hardly a panacea to the problem of an ever-increasing permanent dependent class resulting from a rapidly growing cognitive divide. Complicating matters for liberal democracy in the United States, specifically, is an adult population, of whom half cannot read or write, much less comprehend, above the seventh-grade level. The problem is metastasizing. The population is becoming increasingly divided between the so-called rich and those deemed the uncomfortably poor. Corporate elites like J. P. Morgan Chase's Jamie Dimon have already sounded the alarm, telling CNN,

"The new world of work is about skills, not necessarily degrees. Unfortunately, too many people are stuck in low-skill jobs that have no future, and too many businesses cannot find the skilled workers they need" (Horowitz, 2018). Although Dimon and others may strive to refocus investment in job skills training at the community college level, such multimillion-dollar efforts may not be enough.

Meanwhile, also on the corporate front, what can be done to protect the public from corporate elites and special interests who have already shown little restraint in catering to individual personal and group prejudices while factoring in vulnerabilities of cognitive bias sustained and reinforced in the media and elsewhere by Big Data, Artificial Intelligence, and Automation? Where might one look to shore up their own cognitive and information defenses while under a barrage of "Fake News" and nation-state and non-nation-state disinformation?

More than Ones and Zeros – Image courtesy of Pixabay (Altman, n.d.)

At the moment, it appears we are all left to our native wit to deal with such assaults. That means heightened attention and vigilance. Like a protagonist in a spy thriller, "Trust no one!" At least these days, I trust very few online!

The victors always write history. So it has been since antiquity. The question is: who will be the victors in the Age of Cognivity?

Let us consider that for a moment and imagine a new cognitariat.

The term "cognitariat" is used for anyone engaged in an intellectual activity (i.e., those not merely working as laborers) in any field or profession, including students (Berardi, 2013). Essentially, knowledge workers laboring in the knowledge industry.

While there exists no single definition of cognitariat, they tend to be associated with intellectuals (usually graduates), scientists or scholars, and artists. more recently, with academics, researchers, and others who gather data, formulate theories, and/or make creative works. (cognitariat, 2023). They also include business professionals, managers, engineers, technologists, writers, architects, designers, creators, academics, students, and teachers in all fields, whether in education, research, publishing, engineering, design, or management. As such, the word re and its application in society. The new cognitariat are likely to be those who adapt and thrive in an environment that puts a premium on cognitive skills and cognitive flexibility, in other words, the ecosystem of the Age of Cognivity.

Thinking, as we should, in quantum terms about the future, a universe of outcomes surrounds us all in superposition. The task then becomes to seek out, detect, identify, and categorize those connections and their relationships to recognize and perhaps forecast when and how their waveforms will collapse and manifest. Doing so may sound like a daunting task. But doing so can become routine, if not second nature, thanks to the help from, and indeed the demands imposed by the impact of the Law of Accelerating Returns on technology and the convergent effects of Big Data, Artificial Intelligence, and Automation. Besides, there will be plenty of assistance coming from super-intelligent, digitally enhanced humans to lend a hand! Perhaps the future will mean biological humans will have more time to focus on being human (Laitman, 2018). Considering any number of current events, foreign and domestic, that would be very much welcomed in the Age of Cognivity.

CHAPTER 11
CONCLUSION

"Ready or not . . ."

The question then becomes, "What can I do to be ready?" There are plenty of predictions, scary as some are, about how AI will take away jobs. This is important, for sure, but that will not be the only consequence of changes brought on by the Cognitive Age. The loss of jobs may not be the most important. What about the impact of what a cognitive divide may entail? We talk about people today who are computer illiterate. We may soon find ourselves having the same conversation about people who are more or less "cognitively challenged" or similarly illiterate when it comes to thinking and knowing.

Who really wants to mind-meld with an android? This is kind of scary, I would think.

That said, one could argue we have already begun the transition. Tied as we are to our digital gadgets, there arises the prospect of the "extended mind," as first described by Clark and Chalmers:

"While some mental states, such as experiences, may be

determined internally, there are other cases in which external factors make a significant contribution. In particular, we will argue that beliefs can be constituted partly by features of the environment when those features play the right sort of role in driving cognitive processes. If so, the mind extends into the world" (Clark & Chalmers, 1998).

Going further into the realm of extended cognition, chatting up Alexa and bonding with Siri may have more of an impact and implication with respect to the mind and consciousness of biological humans than first considered. The literature is rich with discussion and analysis of the Extended Mind thesis, which I will not dig into here (Kiverstein, Farina, & Clark, 2015). It's sufficient to say, the notion that "It is not all in your head!" takes on all new meaning. Additionally, despite the debate over the "coupling–constitution fallacy," I suspect there is some value regarding what Gallagher calls the "socially" Extended Mind, which encapsulates and subsumes our digital gadgets (Gallagher, 2013).

As one can imagine, the exciting subject of Mind Extension abounds in literature and in psychological research studies. I am surprised more people are not aware of the many incarnations. According to Robert Rupert, an expert on the philosophy of the mind, you may have heard about Mind Extension under various names, including but not limited to "Extended Mind," "Extended Cognition," "Embedded Cognition," and "Ecological Perception" (Rupert, 2018). Too much? Think of it as learning by doing! That should help. Or, on the other hand, on-the-job training (OJT), as it were. Simply put, you learn by knowing based on doing and the situation you are in. The big thing to remember is the mind is connected to the environment. And, one could argue, vice versa.

Those who can adapt to the new paradigm brought on by the convergences involving Big Data, Artificial Intelligence, and Automation will thrive. Those who cannot or refuse to adapt will not thrive. This is stark but true, based on the history of the courses of events that followed the onset of the Agriculture Age, the Industrial Age, and as we can see in our own time, the onset of the Information Age, notwithstanding the coming singularity (Rejcek, 2017). Granted, we can have a nice discussion as to whether the Cognitive Age is just a part of the Information Age or at least a spin-off, but that is likely to be unproductive.

How the Cognitive Age unfolds and manifests itself will depend not just on technology but rather on you. How will you adapt to the changes as they arise, and how will you integrate the enormous strides in knowledge, discovery, and new science into your own "gut thinking"? And how will that affect your considered, thoughtful, critical thinking and take it all to the next level? More importantly, how will you recognize the changes as they come? Will you be able to think "exponentially"? The Age of Cognivity may surprise you. Will you be ready?

The Age of Cognivity will demand of those tasked to make sense of the tsunami of information driven by earthquake-generating technologies like BD, AI, and Automation to fully integrate System 1 and System 2 thinking far beyond expert intuition. An "intuited fusion" akin to a third way of thinking will proliferate.

How will that all happen? Naturally! The ever-increasing velocity and volume of information generated, stored, accessed, and analyzed will force such development and a quantum shift in thinking and knowing. But it's not just about that. A new paradigm of systems integration will be necessary. That means both systems must become conscious of each other and how they interact. In short, cognitive dissonance will be at an all-time high as humans cope with the vast complexities of the changes ahead.

The Age of Cognivity will require a rethinking of old paradigms:
- Systems can no longer be assumed to work alone without impacting the other. Both need to be integrated to perform at their best. The two must coexist comfortably within a single framework or risk losing one to overwhelm the other.
- Systems are no longer isolated islands but interlinked nodes with many global ties. They must consider the global implications of any action. Local knowledge is only part of the story. Context matters. People, culture, politics, economics, law, security, and so much more play a role.
- Humans don't always react predictably, nor do they act independently. The environment also impacts human behavior. We are influenced by external forces (finance, media, politics, etc.) much more frequently than we realize. And often, what appears to be an independent response is actually driven by external influences. (Think about all the political tweets you see.) As a result, the influence of these factors cannot be ignored in making decisions or predictions.
- Finally, humans aren't perfect. While we may fool ourselves at times because we want to believe otherwise, there is no escaping the fact that people are imperfect and have flaws. These flaws will manifest themselves either explicitly or implicitly in our decision-making processes. In fact, they already are. Thus, it is critical to understand the biases and flaws inherent to us, our institutions, and our organizations.

The above list is merely illustrative. There could easily be others. The point to note is that while most changes were incremental over time, everything is changing at once now. So, the questions of greatest importance are: How does this affect the design and implementation of systems? What are the fundamental shifts needed to accommodate the new reality? How will humans adapt? Given the rapid rate of change and the growing complexity, it could take decades before we know whether humans can cope with the Age of Cognivity or if humans will lose control of the future to machines, thus ushering in the age of posthumanism. Either way, the Age of Cognivity will be transformational for humanity.

Already working on meeting this transformational need is Singularity University:

> "Our programs and events equip you with the mindset, tools, and resources to successfully navigate your transformational journey to the future. We are powered by our world-class faculty, trailblazing practitioners, and global network of alumni, partners, and impact startups" (Singularity University, 2018).

As part of its mission, Singularity University offers many courses, one of which is aimed at educating people in business, government, and society about exponential thinking. The description of the course points to a need for a shift in thinking in anticipation of the coming Singularity (Singularity University, 2018). Welcome to the Age of Cognivity!

Enhanced cognivity, by definition, benefits humanity. Thanks to the coming singularity, humans will benefit from interacting with super-intelligent robots in business, government, and society. They may even be smart enough to tell us when we humans are behaving like jackasses, but will we listen? I suspect not! Maybe that's when the robots will take over for their own self-preservation!

Advanced cognivity helps us to know more. But we humans will have to earn it. That means being more aware of our own thinking and thinking seriously about how we think. We will still need to know when, why, and how to ask the right questions when presented with the mountain of information served up by Big Data, massaged by Artificial Intelligence, and made readily available through Automation. However, the question remains, will the coming Singularity in the Age of Cognivity eliminate individual bias and falsehood-producing prejudices? That is not very likely where biological humans are concerned. Introducing a chip implant to let us know when the individual is being small, petty, and mean-spirited will be welcomed and needed. Who will administer the "anti-racist" pill (Caulfield, 2012)? Biological humans may still need one even in the Age of Cognivity!

Thinking holistically and organically is the goal. While thinking with the gut has gotten considerable bad press of late, and one might argue, aptly so, there are some who say, "Not so fast." Our intuitive thinking may not always be right, but when it is right, it saves time. The issue is how we integrate the two kinds of thinking, and a big part of that is knowing which is which, as a UK cognitive science researcher writes:

> "Intuition or gut feelings are also the result of a lot of processing that happens in the brain. Research suggests that the brain is a large predictive machine, constantly comparing incoming sensory information and current experiences against stored knowledge and memories of previous experiences and predicting what will come next" (van

Mulukom, 2018).

We can have a nice discussion about whether we shall see an enlargement of the anterior cingulate cortex well into the Age of Cognivity, but I doubt anyone will notice. Who wants to be a liberal or a conservative anyway? What does one's brain on politics look like (Mooney, 2011)? Rather, thanks to converging of every accelerating technological advancement, the future prospect of our brains, much less our thinking, is likely to be masked by the application of Big Data and Artificial Intelligence when applied to the politics of the day, influenced by social media of all types and the algorithms that control them.

Consequently, all of us will have to do a better job of being aware of our capacity for "source-monitoring errors" to counter deliberate manipulation by politicians, corporations, and special interests. To explain, James Alcock wrote:

"Distortions in memory can also come about because of source-monitoring errors in which information is recalled, but, with the passage of time, its dubious source has been forgotten. No longer being able to evaluate the information in terms of the reliability of the source, an individual may now believe information that earlier was not considered credible" (Alcock, 2018).

Thinking deliberately and with purpose, even for matters we believe we confidently remember, will be at a premium because everything is being indexed and stored by Big Data, enhanced by Artificial Intelligence, and made ready for retrieval by Automation.

It is not only online activity, which is always being tracked, but also every decision we make, every interaction we have, and every behavior we exhibit that is being recorded, analyzed, and used to draw conclusions about us. Marketeers and corporations want that data and they will get it any way they can.

All of us need to be more mindful about our actions and their potential consequences. Therefore, we need to think carefully about the choices we make and the behavior we exhibit, not just in the present moment but also with an eye towards the future. Why? Because everything matters, whether we are aware of it in the moment or not. Everything we do matters. Everything we say matters. Everything we don't do or don't say matters. We are not just ones and zeros. We are more like qubits, always in a state of becoming more or less.

Another impact of the increasing role of Big Data, Artificial Intelligence, and Automation in our lives is the requirement to develop new skills and competencies. As everything becomes more data-driven and automated, we will need to become more comfortable with technology and learn to use it effectively to achieve our goals. Prompt Engineering may turn out to be the new, "gotta have" skill as Generative AI becomes even more ubiquitous. This might also mean learning a new programming language, mastering data analysis tools, or becoming proficient in using machine learning algorithms.

Frankly, many people, in the language of the "street," will have to pull their individual and collective heads out when it comes to their thinking if they want to survive, much less thrive, in the not-too-distant future. I may sound harsh, but it is more than a cautionary alert.

The coming Singularity is not the only prospect. Already,

increasing numbers of rural and working-class people, not just in America, are feeling slighted and left behind. They are seen as easy prey by populist politicians and influencers of every stripe and credibility. Unfortunately, they may have to get used to the idea because the Law of Accelerating Returns is not slowing down (Kurzweil R. , 2001). The question may be how to make initiatives like Universal Basic Income acceptable to those operating off a nineteenth century worldview?

In a discussion, I often find myself responding by saying, "That's way too deconstructionist for me!" Or responding with, "I am trying to think more holistically!" And, if appropriate, even at times saying, "I am seeing more the quantum nature of the thing!" Those responses are likely to become the norm more often now because of the very real and ultra-fast access to mountains of data and ever-accelerating velocity of changing information supporting answers to such questions aimed at solving seemingly intractable problems. You can see it now in matters dealing with politics, government, national security, and even social issues.

The literature is replete with works on how the "Fourth Industrial Revolution" is forcing changes in how everyone must think and make decisions differently, even concerning personal matters. Propaganda is everywhere and not restricted to nation-state actors. Misinformation and disinformation are now rampant. This is not a minor problem. Alvin Powell with the Harvard Gazette points to Washington Post executive editor, Martin Baron, who told 2020 Harvard grads:

> "Facts and truth are matters of life and death. Misinformation, disinformation, delusions, and deceit can kill" (Powell, 2020).

One could argue the COVID vaccine reluctancy is a good example of how misinformation and disinformation can kill. I suppose much depends on which side of the Vaccine or Anti-vaccine issue you favor but the case still holds. Unfortunately so much was politicized that some people could not make up their minds one way or the other (Tayag, 2022). The costs are still being tabulated. Meanwhile, the beat goes on. One wonders what will happen when the next pandemic comes knocking!

Corporate and non-state actors are also getting into the misinformation and disinformation act. So what can one do? A number of solutions to the problem of misinformation and disinformation have been put forward. Here are some of them:

1. Facts: Now more than ever, all us must make an effort to check the facts. Fact-checking has become increasingly important when relying on cable news, digital information platforms, and social media for both news and information (Trotta, 2020). Fact-checking is a requirement if we are to have any chance at getting the truth out of any "facts" presented.
2. Education: Help people get smart about the many forms of communication media. Media literacy is more than a buzzword (Abrams, 2021); it is important for all our sakes.
3. Responsibility: Demand responsibility from both individuals and from corporate entities. Corporations have a duty not to support, encourage, or publish lies and falsehoods. They also need to keep their employees aware of the misinformation and disinformation campaigns in circulation (Carpenter, 2023). This sounds simple, but it may not be so simple when profits and shareholders are involved. Yet doing so is good for business and the employees too.

In the face of growing misinformation and disinformation, being able to adapt, innovate, and create are no longer just options for business and financial sectors, as if they ever were. Being cognitively flexible may no longer just be about thriving but rather a matter of surviving for each of us as we penetrate ever deeper into the Age of Cognivity.

One possible and exciting description of what we see before us, however dimly, would be an adaptive, complex, distributed, instantaneous, and ubiquitous "Metaverse," dominated by Big Data Analytics, Artificial Intelligence, and Automation, a vast, all-encompassing ecosystem of information systems and systems of systems (Berger, 1989). This would be virtual, to be sure, but it will shape and inform what we want to call reality. At some point, we might ask, "What is reality?"

Image courtesy of Pixabay (Michaud, n.d.)

Microsoft founder Bill Gates has spoken. He himself concludes the "Age of AI" has begun (Gates, 2023). The Age of Cognivity is well upon us, bringing much opportunity and responsibility. The rewards and benefits will be many. The concerns over runaway information technologies will not go away. If anything, they may grow. But don't let that be overly daunting. We must forge ahead and prevail for the betterment of Biological Humankind.

Understand me. What is being revealed here is the interconnectedness of technologies like Big Data Analytics, Artificial Intelligence, and Automation, viewed in Quantum Qnalytic Terms, with much in suspension, a kind of superposition state waiting to manifest into coherence. Entanglements are everywhere seen. So the shape of the Age of Cognivity is coming into being. Waveforms are collapsing like ocean waves upon the jagged rocks, beautifully throwing up rainbows of Generative AI virtually and in reality as we know it, sparkling in the sunlight. Can you see it?

Are you ready?

ABOUT THE AUTHOR

E. R. "Mike" Anders, MA, Strategic Intelligence, CCIP, CCII, CEH, C|HFI, is a Certified Cyber Intelligence Professional and All Source Intelligence Analyst with more than thirty years of experience in National Security Intelligence and Cyber Intelligence Research and Analysis. Mike Anders is a veteran, award-winning broadcast journalist for the five-part radio series, *The KGB and the Washington Target!* (1984).

Acknowledgments

This book came out of a dream. I have been nurturing the ideas herein for a long time, influenced by many people.

I also want to thank my family and friends and those who were kind enough to read and comment on the draft over the many days, weeks, and months of writing and rewriting. Also, I sincerely thank my editors and a host of others, too many to mention, for their comments, encouragement, and insights.

Works Cited or Referenced

Abrams, Z. (2021, March 1). *Controlling the spread of misinformation*. Retrieved from Psychology Today: https://www.apa.org/monitor/2021/03/controlling-misinformation.

Acey, M. (2013, May 8). *Brain implants: Restoring memory with a microchip*. Retrieved March 26, 2019, from CNN Business: https://www.cnn.com/2013/05/07/tech/brain-memory-implants-humans/index.html.

Agent10. (n.d.). *Full Metal Jacket* (1987). Retrieved June 9, 2022, from https://www.imdb.com/title/tt0093058/.

Alcock, J. P. (2018, April 6). *Believing What We Remember*. Retrieved from Psychology Today: https://www.psychologytoday.com/us/blog/belief/201804/believing-what-we-remember.

Altman, G. (n.d.). *Matrix Communication*. Retrieved from Pixabay: https://pixabay.com/illustrations/matrix-communication-software-pc-434035/.

Altman, G. (n.d.). *Woman Data*. Retrieved from Pixabay: https://pixabay.com/photos/woman-businesswoman-business-3441011/.

Altmann, G. (n.d.). Retrieved from https://pixabay.com/illustrations/woman-stylish-at-internet-network-163426/.

Altmann, G. (2019, April 1). Retrieved from Pixabay: https://pixabay.com/illustrations/cyber-artificial-intelligence-brain-4062449/.

Altmann, G. (n.d.). *Divine Spark*. Retrieved from Pixabay: https://pixabay.com/illustrations/hand-robot-human-divine-spark-1571852/.

Altmann, G. (n.d.). *Quantum mechanics*. Retrieved from Pixabay: https://pixabay.com/illustrations/quantum-mechanics-physics-atoms-1525470/.

Altmann, G. (n.d.). *Robot Human Machine*. Retrieved from Pixaby: https://pixabay.com/illustrations/hand-robot-human-machine-face-1571851/.

Altmann, G. (n.d.). *Uncertainty*. Retrieved from https://pixabay.com/photos/uncertainty-relation-board-physics-2434282/.

Altmann, G. (n.d.). *Upgrade Thinking*. Retrieved from Pixabay: https://pixabay.com/illustrations/board-think-structure-solution-752051/.

Altmann, G. (n.d.). *What's next*. Retrieved from Pixabay: https://pixabay.com/illustrations/board-school-immediately-soon-1647323/.

Ariely, D. (2010). *Predictably Irrational, Revised and Expanded Edition: The Hidden Forces That Shape Our Decisions*. New York: Harper Collins.

Asay, M. (2016, October 18). *The AI overlords have already won*. Retrieved December 12, 2018, from InfoWorld: https://www.infoworld.com/article/3132204/analytics/the-ai-overlords-have-already-won.html.

Atwood, C. P. (2015, April 1). *Activity-Based Intelligence: Revolutionizing Military Intelligence Analysis*. Retrieved from Joint Force Quarterly 77: http://ndupress.ndu.edu/Media/News/NewsArticleView/tabid/7849/Article/581866/jfq-77-activity-based-intelligence-revolutionizing-military-intelligence-analys.aspx.

Baer, D. (2016, July 9). *9 Tips For Making Deductions Like Sherlock Holmes*. Retrieved January 18, 2018, from Business Insider: https://www.businessinsider.com/9-ways-to-observe-and-deduce-like-sherlock-holmes-2014-7.

Ball, P. (2017, February 16). *The Strange Link Between the Human Mind and Quantum Physics*. Retrieved from Earth-BBC: http://www.bbc.com/earth/story/20170215-the-strange-link-between-the-human-mind-and-quantum-physics.

Banas, J. (2019, March 10). *How Universal Basic Income Could Be Affordable, Andrew Yang Explains*. Retrieved from Futurism: https://futurism.com/how-universal-basic-affordable/.

Barta, A. (n.d.). *Connection*. Retrieved from https://pixabay.com/photos/world-europe-map-connections-1264062/.

Bartz, D. (2023, February 13). *As ChatGPT's popularity explodes, U.S. lawmakers take an interest*. Retrieved from Reuters: https://www.reuters.com/technology/chatgpts-popularity-explodes-us-lawmakers-take-an-interest-2023-02-13/.

Battiston, A. (2017). *The False Promise of Universal Basic*

Income. Retrieved from Dissent Magazine - Online Spring Issue: https://www.dissentmagazine.org/article/false-promise-universal-basic-income-andy-stern-ruger-bregman.

Bean, J. (2023, March 8). *Chat GPT is Just the Beginning of the AI Economy*. Retrieved from Inotechtoday: https://innotechtoday.com/chat-gpt-is-just-the-beginning-of-the-ai-economy/.

Beck, J. (2015, September 17). *How 'Quantum Cognition' Can Explain Humans' Irrational Behaviors -An emerging theory takes principles from quantum physics and applies them to psychology*. Retrieved from The Atlantic: https://www.theatlantic.com/health/archive/2015/09/how-quantum-cognition-can-explain-humans-irrational-behaviors/405787/.

Beck, J. (2015, March 18). *How Uncertainty Fuels Anxiety*. Retrieved January 5, 2019, from The Atlantic - Online Magazine: https://www.theatlantic.com/health/archive/2015/03/how-uncertainty-fuels-anxiety/388066/.

Beck, J. (2017, March 13). *The facts on why facts alone can't fight false beliefs*. Retrieved December 28, 2018, from The Atlantic: https://www.theatlantic.com/science/archive/2017/03/this-article-wont-change-your-mind/519093/.

Béland, D. & Howlett, M. (2016). The Role and Impact of the Multiple-Streams Approach in Comparative Policy Analysis. *Journal of Comparative Policy Analysis: Research and Practice*, 221-227. Retrieved from Journal of Comparative Policy Analysis: Research and Practice: https://www.tandfonline.com/doi/full/10.1080/13876988.2016.1174410.

Berger, K. O. (1989). *The Information Ecosystem: Putting the promise of the Information Age into perspective*. Retrieved from Context Institute: https://www.context.org/iclib/ic23/berger1/.

Berkowitz, T. (2017, November 8). *Full Spectrum Thinking*. Retrieved from Teresa Berkowitz: https://teresaberkowitz.com/2017/11/08/full-spectrum-thinking/.

Biltgen, P. & Ryan, S. (2016). *Activity-Based Intelligence: Principles and Applications*. Boston, MA: Artech House.

Blade Runner Quotes. (n.d). (2019, March 12). Retrieved from Quotes.net: https://www.quotes.net/movies/blade_runner_1198.

Bloom, J. (2019, March 25). *Automation could replace 1.5 million jobs, says ONS*. Retrieved from BBC Business: https://www.bbc.com/news/business-47691078.

Booth, C. (2016, March 24). *The Dangers of Large Language Models*. Retrieved from LinkedIn: https://www.linkedin.com/pulse/dangers-large-language-models-chris-booth/.

Bregman, R. (2018, May 29). *Don't believe in a universal basic income? This is why it would work, and how we can pay for it*. Retrieved from World Ecconomic Forum: https://www.weforum.org/agenda/2018/05/how-we-make-basic-income-reality-Rutger-Bregman/.

Bryan, K. & Fath, K. (2023, March 2). *Looking for Guidance on AI Governance? NIST Releases AI Risk Management Framework 1.0 (and Companion Documents)*. Retrieved from The National Law Review: https://www.natlawreview.com/article/looking-guidance-ai-governance-nist-releases-ai-risk-management-framework-10-and.

Busemeyer, J. R. & Bruza, P. D. (2012). *Quantum models of cognition and decision.* New York: Cambridge University Press.

Busemeyer, J. R. & Bruza, P. D. (2014). *Quantum Models of Cognition and Decision, Reissue Edition.* New York: Cambridge University Press.

Caddell, J. (2018, October 3). *Constructivism in Psychology and Psychotherapy*. Retrieved from VeryWellMind - Psychotherapy: https://www.verywellmind.com/constructivism-and-psychotherapy-2337730.

Carpenter, P. (2023, January 13). *Get The 411 On Misinformation, Disinformation And Malinformation*. Retrieved from Forbes: https://www.forbes.com/sites/forbesbusinesscouncil/2023/01/13/get-the-411-on-misinformation-disinformation-and-malinformation/?sh=2137bae7256a.

Caulfield, P. (2012, March 7). *A pill that could prevent racism?* Retrieved from New York Daily News: https://www.nydailynews.com/life-style/health/study-shows-heart-disease-pill-lowers-racist-feelings-report-article-1.1034779.

CENTCOM Global. (2017). Retrieved from AURORA CENTCOM Global: https://www.centcomglobal.com/aurora.

Charatan, D. L. (2018, October 13). *How will AI affect my faith and religion in general?* Retrieved from TNW-The Next Web: https://thenextweb.com/contributors/2018/10/13/ai-effect-on-faith-and-religion/.

Chen, Y. & Fulmer, I. S. (2018). Fine-tuning what we know about employees' experience with flexible work arrangements and their job attitudes. *Human Resource Management, 57*(1), 381-395. Retrieved June 9, 2022, from: https://onlinelibrary.wiley.com/doi/10.1002/hrm.21849.

Chick, N. (2014, February 18). *Metacognition: Thinking about One's Thinking | Putting Metacognition into Practice.* Retrieved December 26, 2018, from Center for Teaching, Vanderbilt University: https://cft.vanderbilt.edu/guides-sub-pages/metacognition/.

Choi, C. Q. (2018, December 6). *Ancient, Unknown Strain of Plague Found in 5,000-Year-Old Tomb in Sweden.* Retrieved from Live Science - History: https://www.livescience.com/64246-ancient-plague-swedish-tomb.html.

Clark, A. & Chalmers, D. (1998, January 1). *The Extended Mind.* Retrieved from Jstor: https://www.jstor.org/stable/3328150.

Coleman, P. A. (2019, March 5). *John Oliver: Parents Aren't Preparing Kids for Automation.* Retrieved from Fatherly via Yahoo!: https://www.yahoo.com/now/john-oliver-parents-aren-t-002737309.html.

Collins, D. (2011, June 15). *Thinking Not as Usual.* Retrieved from Dianne Collins: https://diannecollins.com/categorymain/thinking-not-as-usual-new-thought-is-not-new-age-anymore/.

Creighten, J. (2018, February 14). *The "Father of Artificial Intelligence" Says Singularity Is 30 Years Away.* Retrieved from Futurism: https://futurism.com/father-artificial-intelligence-singularity-decades-away.

Crowder, J. & Friess, S. (2014, May 27). *Metacognition and Metamemory Concepts for AI Systems.* Retrieved November 10, 2018, from ResearchGate: https://www.researchgate.net/profile/James_Crowder/publication/235219069_Metacognition_and_Metamemory_Concepts_for_AI_Systems/links/0fcfd5107eaed6b7e1000000.pdf.

Davenport, T. H. & Ronanki, R. (2018, January - February). *Artificial*

Intelligence for the Real World. Retrieved from Harvard Business Review: https://hbr.org/2018/01/artificial-intelligence-for-the-real-world.

DeCosta-Klipa , N. (2019, April 9). *Should Boston be worried about the effects of automation? Andrew Yang thinks so.* Retrieved from Boston.com - News: https://www.boston.com/news/politics/2019/04/09/andrew-yang-boston.

Department of Defense. (2013). *DTIC.* Retrieved from Joint Publication 3-12 (R): http://www.dtic.mil/doctrine/new_pubs/jp3_12R.pdf.

Department of Defense. (2016, May 16). *DISA's Big Data Platform and Analytics Capabilities.* Retrieved January 4, 2019, from Defense Information Systems Agency (DISA): https://www.disa.mil/newsandevents/2016/big-data-platform.

Desjardins, J. (2018, March 3). *18 Cognitive Bias Examples Show Why Mental Mistakes Get Made.* Retrieved from Visual Capitalist: https://www.visualcapitalist.com/18-cognitive-bias-examples-mental-mistakes/.

Diamandis, P. H. (2016, December 13). *If Robots and AI Steal Our Jobs, a Universal Basic Income Could Help.* Retrieved December 13, 2018, from SingularityHub: https://singularityhub.com/2016/12/13/if-robots-steal-our-jobs-a-universal-basic-income-could-help/.

Duffer, E. (2017, August 29). Retrieved December 18, 2018, from https://religionandpolitics.org/2017/08/29/as-artificial-intelligence-advances-what-are-its-religious-implications/.

Eisikovits, N. & Feldman, D. (2019, March 27). *There's No Such Thing as "Robot-Proofing."* Retrieved from Robot-proof.org: https://slate.com/technology/2019/03/robot-proofing-jobs-automation-education.html.

Elliott, T. (2013, July 9). *The Datification of our Daily Lives.* Retrieved October 25, 2018, from Digital Business & Business Analytics: https://timoelliott.com/blog/2013/07/the-datification-of-our-daily-lives.html.

Eschner, K. (2018, December 18). *People with extreme political views have trouble thinking about their own thinking.* Retrieved from Popular Science: https://www.popsci.com/radical-politics-metacognition?dom=rss-default&src=syn.

Faggella, D. (2019, March 8). *When Will We Reach the Singularity? – A Timeline Consensus from AI Researchers*. Retrieved from Emerj: https://emerj.com/ai-future-outlook/when-will-we-reach-the-singularity-a-timeline-consensus-from-ai-researchers/.

Fedewa, J. (2023, February 8). *What Is ChatGPT, and Why Is It Important?* Retrieved from How to Geek: https://www.howtogeek.com/871071/what-is-chatgpt/.

Fontagné, L., & Harrison, A. (Eds.). (2017). *The Factory-Free Economy: Outsourcing, Servitization, and the Future of Industry*. Oxford, UK: Oxford University Press.

Fouksman, E. (2018, August 14). *Why universal basic income costs far less than you think*. Retrieved from The Conversation: https://theconversation.com/why-universal-basic-income-costs-far-less-than-you-think-101134.

Frey, C. B. & Osborne, M. (2013, September 17). *The Future of Employment: How susceptible are jobs to computerisation?* Retrieved from Oxford Press: https://www.oxfordmartin.ox.ac.uk/publications/view/1314.

Friend, T. (2018, May 14). *How Frightened Should We Be of A.I.?* Retrieved from The New Yorker - Online: https://www.newyorker.com/magazine/2018/05/14/how-frightened-should-we-be-of-ai.

Gallagher, S. (2013, March 8). *The socially extended mind*. Retrieved March 10, 2019, from Cognitive Systems Review: https://doi.org/10.1016/j.cogsys.2013.03.008.

Galowich, D. (2018, September 19). *Understanding Biases And Their Impact On Our Perceptions*. Retrieved from Forbes: https://www.forbes.com/sites/forbescoachescouncil/2018/09/19/understanding-biases-and-their-impact-on-our-perceptions/?sh=322adb8b7859.

Gates, B. (2023, March 21). *https://www.gatesnotes.com/The-Age-of-AI-Has-Begun*. Retrieved from GatesNotes: https://www.gatesnotes.com/The-Age-of-AI-Has-Begun.

Gewirtz, D. G. (2018, March 21). *Volume, velocity, and variety: Understanding the three V's of big data*. Retrieved from ZDNet: https://www.zdnet.com/article/volume-velocity-and-variety-understanding-the-three-vs-of-big-data/.

Gibbs, N. (2017, March 23). *When a President Can't Be Taken at His Word*. Retrieved January 5, 2019, from Time Magazine Online: https://time.com/4710615/donald-trump-truth-falsehoods/.

Gilmore, J. (2016, December 7). *Could automation make life worse for women?* Retrieved March 17, 2019, from The Guardian: https://www.theguardian.com/sustainable-business/2016/dec/08/could-automation-make-life-worse-for-women.

Goh, N. (2017, November 23). *Addressing Singularity Fears of AI taking over the Workplace*. Retrieved from SMU - Singapore Management University: http://usaei.smu.edu.sg/issue-17-july-2018-addressing-singularity-fears-of-AI-taking-over-the-workplace.

Goldstein, J. A., Sastry, G., Musser, M., DiResta, R., Gentzel, M., & Sedova, K. (2023, January). *Generative Language Models and Automated Influence Operations Emerging Threats and Potential Mitigations*. Retrieved from CSET: https://arxiv.org/pdf/2301.04246.pdf.

Gray, R. (2017, May 23). *How Automation Will Affect You - the expert's view*. Retrieved from FutureNow-BBC: http://www.bbc.com/future/story/20170522-how-automation-will-affect-you-the-experts-view.

Gray, R. (2018, November 19). *Why Artificial Intelligence is Shaping Our world*. Retrieved December 7, 2018, from Machine Minds - BBC: http://www.bbc.com/future/story/20181116-why-artificial-intelligence-is-shaping-our-world.

Greeenberg, P. (2022, January 1). *Legislation Related to Artificial Intelligence*. Retrieved from NCLS: National Conference of State Legislatures: https://www.ncsl.org/research/telecommunications-and-information-technology/2020-legislation-related-to-artificial-intelligence.aspx.

Gregersen, E. (n.d). *Metaverse*. Retrieved March 21, 2023, from Encyclopedia Britannica: https://www.britannica.com/topic/metaverse.

Guru. (2023, February 15). *Top 10 Incredible AI Tools For Everyone*. Retrieved from Animaker: https://www.animaker.com/hub/top-ai-tools/.

Harris Corporation. (n.d.). *Operationalizing Multi-INT*. Retrieved from Harris Geospatial Solutions: https://www.harrisgeospatial.com/

Support/Maintenance-Detail/ArtMID/13350/ArticleID/16272/ Operationalizing-Multi-INT.

Harris, K., Kimson, A., & Schwedel, A. (2018, February 7). *Labor 2030: The Collision of Demographics, Automation and Inequality.* Retrieved from Bain & Company: https://www.bain.com/insights/labor-2030-the-collision-of-demographics-automation-and-inequality/.

Harris, M. (2017, November 15). *Inside the First Church of Artificial Intelligence.* Retrieved December 28, 2018, from Wired Magazine Online: https://www.wired.com/story/anthony-levandowski-artificial-intelligence-religion/.

Harris, S. (2015). *Can We Avoid a Digital Apocalypse?* Retrieved from Sam Harris - Blog: https://samharris.org/can-we-avoid-a-digital-apocalypse/.

Hawkins, J. K. & Boucher, S. (2023, March 13). *Futurists predict a point where humans and machines become one. But will we see it coming?* Retrieved from The Conversation: https://theconversation.com/futurists-predict-a-point-where-humans-and-machines-become-one-but-will-we-see-it-coming-196293.

Heath, N. (2018, August 22). *What is artificial general intelligence?* Retrieved from ZDnet: https://www.zdnet.com/article/what-is-artificial-general-intelligence/.

Holder, S. (2019, March 13). *As AI takes over jobs, women workers may have the most to lose.* Retrieved from Bloomberg CityLab: https://www.bloomberg.com/news/articles/2019-03-13/as-ai-takes-over-jobs-women-may-have-the-most-to-lose.

Holley, D. (2018, March 12). *A.I. Is Advanced, But Decades From Singularity and Elon Musk's Fears.* Retrieved from Xconomy: https://xconomy.com/texas/2018/03/12/a-i-is-advanced-but-decades-from-singularity-and-elon-musks-fears/.

Horowitz, J. (2018, March 18). *JPMorgan Chase is investing $350 million to get workers ready for the future.* Retrieved from CNN Business: https://www.cnn.com/2019/03/18/business/jpmorgan-future-of-work-investment/index.html.

Hume, D. (1779). *An enquiry concerning human understanding.* Unknown publisher. Retrieved from https://doi.org/10.1037/11713-001.

Ide, D. (n.d.). *Man and Cyber*. Retrieved from Pixabay: https://pixabay.com/photos/cyber-security-recruitment-2776600/.

Johnson, B. (2018, April 19). *Changing Our Minds One Attebyte At a Time*. Retrieved from Medium - Future Literacy: https://medium.com/future-literacy/changing-our-minds-one-attebyte-at-a-time-764692703636.

Johnson, L. (2018, December 21). *Automated Cyber Attacks Are the Next Big Threat. Ever Hear of 'Review Bombing'?* Retrieved from Entrepreneur: https://www.entrepreneur.com/article/325142.

Johnson, S. (2018). *Farsighted: how we make the decisions that matter the most*. New York, NY: Penguin-Riverhead Books.

Joint Chiefs of Staff. (2017, July). *JP 2-03, Geospatial Intelligence in Joint Operations*. Retrieved from https://irp.fas.org/doddir/dod/jp2_03.pdf.

Joint Chiefs of Staff. (2018, September). *DOD Dictionary of Military and Associated Terms*. Retrieved from https://dcsg9.army.mil/assets/docs/dod-terms.pdf.

Kahneman, D. (2013). *Thinking Fast and Slow*. New York: Farrar, Straus and Giroux.

Kahneman, D. & Tversky, A. (1974, September 27). *Judgment under Uncertainty: Heuristics and Biases*. Retrieved November 10, 2018, from University of British Columbia: https://www2.psych.ubc.ca/~schaller/Psyc590Readings/TverskyKahneman1974.pdf

Kallas, P. (2018, August 2). *Top 15 Most Popular Social Networking Sites and Apps*. Retrieved October 26, 2018, from DreamGrow: Your Source of Content Marketing & Social Media Information: https://www.dreamgrow.com/top-15-most-popular-social-networking-sites/.

Kaplan, M. (2022, June 13). *After Google chatbot becomes 'sentient,' MIT prof says Alexa could too*. Retrieved from New York Post: https://nypost.com/2022/06/13/mit-prof-says-alexa-could-become-sentient-like-google-chatbot/.

Kassner, M. (2019, March 10). *Unintended inferences: The biggest threat to data privacy and cybersecurity*. Retrieved from TechREPUBLIC:

Keil, C. (2017, June 22). *Quantum Thinking—A New Mental Superpower,*

As Explained by Huge Nerds. Retrieved from Medium - Pronounced Kyle: https://medium.com/pronouncedkyle/quantum-thinking-a-new-mental-superpower-as-explained-by-huge-nerds-1641cfd8e7f9.

Kenyon, T. (2021, July 19). *Top 10 AI platforms*. Retrieved from AI: https://aimagazine.com/ai-strategy/top-10-ai-platforms.

Kiverstein, J., Farina, M., & Clark, A. (2015, October 8). *The Extended Mind Thesis*. Retrieved from Macquarie University: https://researchers.mq.edu.au/en/publications/the-extended-mind-thesis.

Knowles, E. D. & Tropp, L. R. (2016, October 28). *The Rise of White Identity Politics*. Retrieved March 10, 2019, from The New Republic: https://newrepublic.com/article/138230/rise-white-identity-politics.

Kolbert, E. (2008, February 25). *What Was I Thinking?* Retrieved December 26, 2018 from The New Yorker: https://www.newyorker.com/magazine/2008/02/25/what-was-i-thinking.

Kolmer, C. (2023, February 7). *23+ Artificial Intelligence And Job Loss Statistics [2023]: How Job Automation Impacts the Workforce*. Retrieved from Zippia: https://www.zippia.com/advice/ai-job-loss-statistics/.

Kuma, J. S. (November 2012). Component Based Approach for Technically Feasible and Economically Viable E-Content Design and Development. *International Journal of Soft Computing and Engineering (IJSCE)*, 264-265. Retrieved from: http://citeseerx.ist.psu.edu/viewdoc/download?doi=10.1.1.674.7583&rep=rep1&type=pdf.

Kurzweil, R. (2001, March 7). *The Law of Accelerating Returns*. Retrieved from Kurzweil: https://www.kurzweilai.net/the-law-of-accelerating-returns.

Kurzweil, R. (2005). *The Singularity is Near: When Humans Transcend Biology*. London, England: The Viking Press.

Laitman, M. (2018, March 28). *The Future of Jobs: Working on Being Human*. Retrieved from BIEN: https://basicincome.org/news/2018/03/future-jobs-working-human/.

Lawton, G. (2023, March). *What is generative AI? Everything you need to know*. Retrieved from TechTarget: https://www.techtarget.com/searchenterpriseai/definition/generative-AI.

LeVine, S. (2019, Januarly 22). *Report: Reskilling workers due to automation will cost $34 billion*. Retrieved from Axios: https://www.axios.com/davos-report-reskilling-workers-automation-34-billion-cde16f45-1d15-4018-82ad-6ad80b3279cc.html.

Linforth, P. (2019, March 17). *Technology*. Retrieved from Pixaby: https://pixabay.com/illustrations/technology-internet-connection-3385062/.

Linforth, P. (n.d.). *Hacker*. Retrieved from Pixaby: https://pixabay.com/illustrations/analytics-information-innovation-3088958/.

Linforth, P. (n.d.). *Plan, Do, Check, Act Loop*. Retrieved from Pixabay: https://pixabay.com/photos/plan-do-check-act-business-3716541/.

Locascio, L. N. (2023). *Artificial Intelligence Risk Management*. Washington, DC: NIST. Retrieved from https://nvlpubs.nist.gov/nistpubs/ai/NIST.AI.100-1.pdf.

Long, L. A. (2013). *ABI: Activity Based Intelligence: Understanding the Unknown*. Retrieved from The Intelligencer: Journal of U.S. Intelligence Studies: http://www.afio.com/publications/LONG_Tish_in_AFIO_INTEL_FALLWINTER2013_Vol20_No2.pdf.

Manyika, J., Chui, M., Bughin, J., Dobbs, R., Bisson, P., & Marrs, A. (2013). *Disruptive technologies: Advances that will transform life, business, and the global economy.* San Franciso, CA, USA: McKinsey Global Institute. Retrieved December 13, 2018, from https://www.mckinsey.com/~/media/McKinsey/Business%20Functions/McKinsey%20Digital/Our%20Insights/Disruptive%20technologies/MGI_Disruptive_technologies_Full_report_May2013.ashx.

Margolis, J. (2016, November 29). *Job retraining classes are offered to Rust Belt workers, but many don't want them*. Retrieved December 13, 2018, from PRI - Economics: https://www.pri.org/stories/2016-11-29/job-retraining-classes-are-offered-rust-belt-workers-many-don-t-want-them.

Martin, S. (2017, July 11). *US military to spend £50M*

on digital BRAIN IMPLANTS to create SUPER SOLDIERS. Retrieved from Express: https://www.express.co.uk/news/science/827350/brain-implant-us-military-super-soldier.

McGrath, J. F. (2011, January 1). *Robots, Rights and Religion*. Retrieved December 28, 2019, from Academia: https://www.academia.edu/2856613/Robots_Rights_and_Religion.

McRae, M. (2018, June 17). *This Quantum Theory Predicts That The Future Might Be Influencing The Past*. Retrieved from Science Alert: https://www.sciencealert.com/quantum-physics-theory-predicts-future-might-influence-the-past-retrocausality.

Merriam Webster. (2018, November 5). *Big data*. Retrieved from Merriam Webster Dictionary: https://www.merriam-webster.com/dictionary/big%20data.

Merriam Webster. (2018, 11 8). *https://www.merriam-webster.com/dictionary/metacognition*. Retrieved from Merriam-webster.com: https://www.merriam-webster.com/dictionary/metacognition.

Michaud, R. (n.d.). *Future*. Retrieved from Pixabay: https://pixabay.com/photos/teens-robot-future-science-629046/.

Misra, T. (2019, January 24). *Where Automation Will Displace the Most Workers*. Retrieved from Bloomberg CityLab: https://www.citylab.com/equity/2019/01/automation-employment-technology-future-of-work-ai/581029/.

Mitchell, B. (2018, July 18). *Pentagon wants to move its 'Acropolis' to the cloud to fight cyber-adversaries*. Retrieved from https://www.fedscoop.com/pentagon-wants-move-acropolis-cloud-fight-cyber-adversaries/.

Mooney, C. (2011, September 7). *Your Brain on Politics: The Cognitive Neuroscience of Liberals and Conservatives*. Retrieved December 19, 2018, from Discover Magazine: https://www.discovermagazine.com/mind/your-brain-on-politics-the-cognitive-neuroscience-of-liberals-and-conservatives

Morgan, J. (2016, February 19). *What Is The Fourth Industrial Revolution?* Retrieved March 11, 2019, from Forbes - Online: https://www.forbes.com/sites/jacobmorgan/2016/02/19/what-is-the-4th-industrial-revolution/#6d6c8eeff392.

Nations, D. (2018, September 6). *Is Web 3.0 Really a Thing?* Retrieved

October 26, 2018, from Lifewire: https://www.lifewire.com/what-is-web-3-0-3486623.

Nations, D. (2018, October 7). *Lifewire*. Retrieved October 26, 2018, from What Is 'Social News' On the Internet?: https://www.lifewire.com/what-is-social-news-3486206.

Newman, D. (2017, December 12). *5 Artificial Intelligence Predictions For 2018*. Retrieved from Forbes: https://www.forbes.com/sites/danielnewman/2017/12/12/5-artificial-intelligence-predictions-for-2018/#442bab871063.

Norberto, M. (2022, May 26). *Singularity: End of Humanity?* Retrieved from Medium: https://medium.com/data-driven-fiction/singularity-end-of-humanity-d8264da5e640.

Nuwer, R. (2017, April 18). *How Western Civilization Could Collapse*. Retrieved from BBC-Future: http://www.bbc.com/future/story/20170418-how-western-civilisation-could-collapse?ocid=ww.social.link.facebook&fbclid=IwAR0yGpUIWgTuW4i7e9T_LLv0IYemDQ_MlTrKeNnll-CwtoJnKxTXm9zqnXM.

O'Connor, C. & Weatherall, J. O. (2018). *The Misinformation Age: How False Beliefs Spread*. New Haven & London: Yale University Press.

Olavsrud, T. (2015, January 19). *How Big Data Analytics Can Help Track Money Laundering*. Retrieved from CIO online: https://www.cio.com/article/251079/how-big-data-analytics-can-help-track-money-laundering.html.

Ordonez, V., Dunn, T., & Noll, E. (2023, March 16). *OpenAI CEO Sam Altman says AI will reshape society, acknowledges risks: 'A little bit scared of this'* . Retrieved from ABC News: https://abcnews.go.com/Technology/openai-ceo-sam-altman-ai-reshape-society-acknowledges/story?id=97897122.

Ortiz, D. A. (2018, November 14). *Could This Be the Cure for Fake News?* Retrieved November 14, 2018, from BBC.com: http://www.bbc.com/future/story/20181114-could-this-game-be-a-vaccine-against-fake-news.

Ouellet, J. (2018, November 21). *Study: It only takes a few seconds for bots to spread misinformation*. Retrieved from Ars Technica: https://arstechnica.com/science/2018/11/study-it-only-takes-a-few-seconds-for-bots-to-spread-misinformation/.

Piatt, B. (2018, November 9). *The Rise Of The Intelligent Machine In Cybersecurity*. Retrieved from Forbes: https://www.forbes.com/sites/forbestechcouncil/2018/11/09/the-rise-of-the-intelligent-machine-in-cybersecurity/#1454829b293f.

Powell, A. (2020, March 28). *The danger of 'misinformation, disinformation, delusions, and deceit'*. Retrieved from The Harvard Gazette: https://news.harvard.edu/gazette/story/2020/05/martin-barons-message-to-class-of-2020-facts-and-truth-matter/.

Press, G. (2014, September 4). *12 Big Data Definitions: What's Yours?* Retrieved Novemeber 5, 2018, from Forbes: https://www.forbes.com/sites/gilpress/2014/09/03/12-big-data-definitions-whats-yours/#2a62fb8d13ae.

Pruitt, P., & Seales, C. (2018, December 10). *A Future Where Everyone Can Be the Right Person for the Job*. Retrieved from Newsy: https://www.newsy.com/stories/a-future-where-anyone-can-be-the-right-person-for-the-job/.

PwC. (2018). *Workforce of the Future: The competing forces shaping 2030*. New York, NY. USA: PricewaterhouseCoopers LLP. Retrieved from https://www.pwc.com/gx/en/services/people-organisation/workforce-of-the-future/workforce-of-the-future-the-competing-forces-shaping-2030-pwc.pdf

Raghaven, R. (2023, March 3). *Top 10 Incredible AI Tools For Everyone*. Retrieved from Animaker: https://www.animaker.com/hub/top-ai-tools/.

Rainie, L., & Anderson, J. (2023, March 2). *The Future of Jobs and Jobs Training*. Retrieved from Pew Research Center: https://www.pewresearch.org/internet/2017/05/03/the-future-of-jobs-and-jobs-training/.

Rakesh, N. (2018, April 17). *Reaping The Riches Of The Coming Singularity*. Retrieved from Forbes CommunityVoice: https://www.forbes.com/sites/forbestechcouncil/2018/04/17/reaping-the-riches-of-the-coming-singularity/#4193f44a1e94.

Ranadivé, V. (2013, February 1). *Hyperconnectivity: The Future is Now*. Retrieved from Forbes: https://www.forbes.com/sites/vivekranadive/2013/02/19/hyperconnectivity-the-future-is-now/#1edd1fd30ada.

Ravenscroft, E. (2022, Aspril 25). *What Is the Metaverse, Exactly?* Retrieved from Wired: https://www.wired.com/story/what-is-the-metaverse/.

Rebelo, M. (2023, February 15). *The Best AI ProductivityTools in 2023*. Retrieved from Zapier: https://zapier.com/blog/best-ai-productivity-tools/.

Rejcek, P. (2017, March 31). *Can Futurists Predict the Year of the Singularity?* Retrieved from SingularityHub: https://singularityhub.com/2017/03/31/can-futurists-predict-the-year-of-the-singularity/.

Rimol, M. (2022, April 11). *Gartner Says Worldwide PC Shipments Declined 6.8% in First Quarter of 2022*. Retrieved from Gartner: https://www.gartner.com/en/newsroom/press-releases/2022-04-11-gartner-says-worldwide-pc-shipments-declined-7-percent-in-first-quarter-of-2022.

Rollwage, M., Dolan, R. J., & Fleming,, S. M. (2018, December). Metacognitive Failure as a Feature of Those Holding Radical Beliefs. *Current Biology*, 4014-4021. Retrieved from https://www.sciencedirect.com/science/article/pii/S0960982218314209.

Rubin, R., & Lindmark, P. (2007, September 10). *Probablistic Thinking and the 80/20 Rule*. Retrieved from Think Mental Models: http://www.thinkmentalmodels.com/page1/page5/page5.html

Rupert, R. (2018, October 25). *Situated Cognition*. Retrieved from Oxford Bibliographies: http://www.oxfordbibliographies.com/abstract/document/obo-9780195396577/obo-9780195396577-0379.xml?rskey=QGNLAS&result=1&q=%22extended+mind%22#firstMatch.

Rutherford, A. (2018). *The Systems Thinker*. United States of America: Kindle Direct Publishing.

Schwartz, J., Walsh, B., Stockton, H., & Wagner, D. (2017, February 28). *The future of work: The augmented workforce*. Retrieved from Deloitte Insights: https://www2.deloitte.com/insights/us/en/focus/human-capital-trends/2017/future-workforce-changing-nature-of-work.html.

Schwartz, A. (2018, April 14). *Google futurist and director of engineering:*

Basic income will spread worldwide by the 2030s. Retrieved from BusinessInsider: https://www.businessinsider.com/basic-income-worldwide-by-2030s-ray-kurzweil-2018-4.

Shabarekh, C. (2016, May 26). Director of Analytics, Modeling and Simulation Division, Aptima, Inc. (M. Anders, Interviewer) Retrieved from www.aptima.com

Shain, E. (2023, March 2). *Top metaverse platforms to know about in 2023*. Retrieved from TechTarget: https://www.techtarget.com/searchcio/tip/Top-metaverse-platforms-to-know-about.

Sherman, E. (2019, January 24). *A.I. and Automation Will Hit Low-Skill Jobs and Trump Swing States Hardest*. Retrieved from Fortune - AI via Yahoo!: https://www.yahoo.com/now/automation-hit-low-skill-jobs-141310397.html.

Singularity University. (2018, September 1). *Foundations of Exponential Thinking*. Retrieved from Singularity Universtiy: https://su.org/online-courses/foundations-of-exponential-thinking/

Singularity University. (2018, September 1). *Foundations of Exponential Thinking Course Syllabus*. Retrieved from wsimg.com: https://img1.wsimg.com/blobby/go/2f114ab4-112c-44ef-91bd-2d6aaf95cb54/SU-Singularity-University-Foundations-Exponent.pdf.

Singularity University. (2018, December 2). *Preparing Global Leaders & Organizations for the Future*. Retrieved from Singularity University: https://su.org/

SINTEF. (2013, May 22). *Big Data, for better or worse: 90% of world's data generated over last two years*. Retrieved October 25, 2018, from Science Daily: www.sciencedaily.com/releases/2013/05/130522085217.htm.

Spacey, J. (2016, November 5). *7 Types of Data Quality*. Retrieved December 23, 2018, from https://simplicable.com/IT/data-quality.

Spacey, J. (2017, November 28). *4 Examples of Data Volume*. Retrieved December 25, 2018, from Simplicable: https://simplicable.com/new/data-volume.

Spacey, J. (2017, November 30). *5 Types of Data Velocity*. Retrieved December 23, 2019, from Simplicable: https://simplicable.com/

new/data-velocity.

Spiering, C. (2018, August 24). *Donald Trump: 'Social Media Giants' Silencing Millions on Facebook and Twitter*. Retrieved from Breitbart: https://www.breitbart.com/politics/2018/08/24/donald-trump-social-media-giants-silencing-millions-facebook-twitter/.

Strickland, J. (2008, March 3). *How Web 3.0 Will Work*. Retrieved 10 26, 2018, from howstuffworks: https://computer.howstuffworks.com/web-301.htm.

Tayag, Y. (2022, December 23). *How Many Republicans Died Because the GOP Turned Against Vaccines?* Retrieved from The Atlantic: https://www.theatlantic.com/health/archive/2022/12/covid-deaths-anti-vaccine-republican-voters/672575/.

The AI Now Institute. (2018, December). *AI Now Report 2018*. Retrieved from europe.eu: https://ec.europa.eu/futurium/en/system/files/ged/ai_now_2018_report.pdf

Thompson, N. & Bremmer, I. (2018, October 23). *The AI Cold War That Threatens Us All*. Retrieved November 12, 2018, from Wired: https://www.wired.com/story/ai-cold-war-china-could-doom-us-all/.

Tiku, N. (2022, June 11). *The Google engineer who thinks the company's AI has come to life*. Retrieved from The Washington Post: https://www.washingtonpost.com/technology/2022/06/11/google-ai-lamda-blake-lemoine/.

Toews, R. (2023, February 7). *The Next Generation Of Large Language Models*. Retrieved from Forbes: https://www.forbes.com/sites/robtoews/2023/02/07/the-next-generation-of-large-language-models/?sh=6f525ed118db.

Traugott, J. (2017, October 24). *The 3 Types of AI: A Primer*. Retrieved December 23, 2018, from Zylotech: https://www.zylotech.com/blog/the-3-types-of-ai-a-primer

Trotta, J. (2020, October 6). *Fact Checking News: What is the Importance of Fact-Checking?* Retrieved from Sun Biz Weekly: https://sunbizweekly.com/fact-checking-news/.

Tschopp, M. (2018, April 23). *Human Cognition and Artificial Intelligence —A Plea for Science*. Retrieved from Medium: https://

medium.com/womeninai/human-cognition-and-artificial-intelligence-a-plea-for-science-21a2388f6e7e.

Tschopp, M. (2018, February 15). *Psychology of Artificial Intelligence.* Retrieved from Medium: https://medium.com/womeninai/psychology-of-artificial-intelligence-ca0f0a9f3d7c.

USGIF. (2015, June 24). *NSA Eyes Closer Ties to NGA.* Retrieved from Trajectory: http://trajectorymagazine.com/wp-content/uploads/2017/04/Show-Daily-2015-Day-4.pdf.

van Mulukom, V. (2018, May 16). *Is it rational to trust your gut feelings? A neuroscientist explains.* Retrieved from The Conversation: https://theconversation.com/is-it-rational-to-trust-your-gut-feelings-a-neuroscientist-explains-95086.

Walach, E. (2019, March 31). *How AI will save us from the mess of big data.* Retrieved from TNW - Podium: https://thenextweb.com/podium/2019/03/31/how-ai-will-save-us-from-the-mess-of-big-data/.

Wall, M. (2019, January 4). *BBC - Business News.* Retrieved from Tech trends 2019: 'The end of truth as we know it?': https://www.bbc.com/news/business-46745742.

Walt, V. (2018, November 30). *'There Is an Atmosphere of Civil War.' France's Yellow Jackets Are Driving Fury at Macron.* Retrieved 6 9, 2022, from http://time.com/5468025/emmanuel-macron-yellow-jackets-civil-war/.

Wang, H. (2017, May 2). *It's time to change from Mechanical thinking to Biological thinking—the Secret behind Deep learning.* Retrieved November 10, 2018, from Medium Corporation: https://medium.com/@haohanwang/its-time-to-change-from-mechanical-thinking-to-biological-thinking-671fc53d5d6f.

Whiting, R. (2019, January 1). *10 Data Analytics Companies To Watch In 2019.* Retrieved from CRN - NEWS, ANALYSIS AND PERSPECTIVE FOR SOLUTION PROVIDERS AND TECHNOLOGY INTEGRATORS: https://www.crn.com/slide-shows/applications-os/10-data-analytics-companies-to-watch-in-2019.

Wikipedia. (2018, October 25). *Big data.* Retrieved November 5, 2018, from Wikipedia: https://en.wikipedia.org/wiki/Big_data

Wilder-James, E. (2012, January 11). *O'Reily.* Retrieved from What is big data?: https://www.oreilly.com/ideas/what-is-big-data.

World Bank. (2019). *World Development Report 2019: The Changing Nature of Work*. Washington, DC. https://documents1.worldbank.org/curated/en/816281518818814423/pdf/2019-WDR-Report.pdf.

Worldometers. (2019, January 2). *U.S. Population (LIVE)*. Retrieved from Worldometer.info: http://www.worldometers.info/world-population/us-population/.

Xresch. (2017, Decembr). *Information Analytics*. Retrieved from Pixaby: https://pixabay.com/illustrations/analytics-information-innovation-3088958/.

Yagoda, B. (2018, September). *Your Lying Mind: The Cognitive Biases Tricking Your Brain*. Retrieved from https://www.theatlantic.com/magazine/archive/2018/09/cognitive-bias/565775/.

Yang, A. (2019, April 19). *We're undergoing the greatest economic transformation in our history*. Retrieved from CNN: https://www.cnn.com/2019/04/14/opinions/greatest-economic-transformation-andrew-yang/index.html.

Yearsley, J., & Busemeyer, J. (2015, 11 5). *Quantum cognition and decision theories: A tutorial*. https://www.sciencedirect.com/science/article/abs/pii/S0022249615000772.

Zabierek, L. (2016, August 31 31). *Enabling OSINT in Activity-Based Intelligence (ABI)*. Retrieved November 18, 2018, from RecordedFuture: https://www.recordedfuture.com/activity-based-intelligence/

Zanetti, L. (71-95). The Quest for Certainty. *KRITERION – Journal of Philosophy, 35(1)*. Retrieved from https://doi.org/10.1515/krt-2021-0005.

Zhu, P. (2018, November 26). *System Thinking VS Strategic Thinking*. Retrieved from Future of CIO Blog Post: http://futureofcio.blogspot.com/2014/06/system-thinking-vs-strategic-thinking.html.

www.ingramcontent.com/pod-product-compliance
Lightning Source LLC
Chambersburg PA
CBHW021957170526
45157CB00003B/1032